21
DAYS TO

Master
Numerology

Also in the 21 Days series

21
DAYS TO

Master
Numerology

Understand Your Inner Self and
Find Your True Purpose with
Your Birth Chart

DAVID A. PHILLIPS

HAY HOUSE

Carlsbad, California • New York City
London • Sydney • New Delhi

Published in the United Kingdom by:
Hay House UK Ltd, The Sixth Floor, Watson House,
54 Baker Street, London W1U 7BU
Tel: +44 (0)20 3927 7290; www.hayhouse.co.uk

Published in the United States of America by:
Hay House Inc., PO Box 5100, Carlsbad, CA 92018-5100
Tel: (1) 760 431 7695 or (800) 654 5126; www.hayhouse.com

Published in Australia by:
Hay House Australia Pty Ltd, 18/36 Ralph St, Alexandria NSW 2015
Tel: (61) 2 9669 4299; www.hayhouse.com.au

Published in India by:
Hay House Publishers India, Muskaan Complex,
Plot No.3, B-2, Vasant Kunj, New Delhi 110 070
Tel: (91) 11 4176 1620; www.hayhouse.co.in

A catalogue record for this book is available from the British Library.

Tradepaper ISBN: 978-1-78817-907-2
E-book ISBN: 978-1-78817-921-8
Audiobook ISBN: 978-1-78817-862-4

MIX
Paper from
responsible sources
FSC
www.fsc.org   FSC® C013056

Contents

Publisher's Note

Research has shown that establishing a habit requires 21 days' practice. That's why Hay House has decided to adapt the work of some of its most prestigious authors into these short, 21-day courses, designed specifically to develop new mastery of subjects such as numerology.

21 Days to Master Numerology draws from David A. Phillips's best-selling *The Complete Book of Numerology* (Hay House, 2006).

Some references in this book have been updated to reflect the modern world we now live in. However, David's voice and message have been strictly preserved.

Note: the date formats used in this book are in US style (month/day/year).

Other titles that will help you to further explore the concepts featured in the 21-day program are listed at the beginning of this book.

Introduction

My life radically changed when I met Hettie Templeton in 1954. Not quite sure of my career choice to be an electrical engineer, my friend Bill Christopher suggested I see Mrs T. and "have your numbers read."

Though my student days were devoted to the use of numbers, to comparing quantities and solving equations, I was yet to be convinced that numbers could be used to unravel life's problems. Yet within five minutes of meeting Mrs T., my doubt dissolved.

Equipped with only my birth date and my name, Mrs T. told me things about myself that I thought only I knew. That hour with her changed my life's direction. It gave me a confidence I had not previously known and explained many "mysterious" past events. I was fascinated. So the following year, coinciding with my postgraduate research into medical electronics, I commenced study in numerology, the Science of Numbers.

Over the many long years that I have studied numerology, I've learned that there is no better way for us to understand ourselves, or our personal connections with others.

So many people spend so much of their time zigzagging through life, bouncing from experience to experience as though caught in a pinball machine. We simply do not know our own minds, nor the appropriate path(s) to take. And though there are countless courses and seminars available today devoted to personal growth, the information overload often creates psychological and intellectual indigestion—and a whole new experience of inner confusion.

Numerology, on the other hand, provides direct knowledge of the inner self, and from this basis of self-understanding, we are able to direct a determined course through life.

Numerology recognizes that numbers are vibrations, and each vibration is different from the next due to the number of cycles it oscillates at per second. The variation in each case is a number. Every sound, color, fragrance, and thought is a vibration, and each dances to the tune of its inherent number, each in its distinct way connected to life. Thus, it doesn't take too much imagination to realize that human life has an intimate connection with numbers, for they are the very essence of life's expression.

As such, understanding numbers provides us with a simple and accurate meaning of our life in the same way as a road map helps us to navigate a route we have not previously traveled.

Within each person is a beautiful light waiting to shine forth, a magnificent being aching for expression. That is the inner self, our individuality, our essential uniqueness. But this is not what we generally present to the world. Instead we have produced a "personality," a composite expression at the crux of which is our individuality (our inner self).

The average person is often two people. That which is freely expressed is usually the image, while the real person, the unique individuality of our inner self, is all too frequently suppressed. The image is something of an emotional ghost we have cultivated to defend our sensitivities. But we sell ourselves far too short, for our image can never hold to the beauty and grandeur of our natural inner self.

The acute sensitivity of the inner self is often mistaken for vulnerability and, as a consequence, we build up a psychological wall. We stifle it, refusing to give it air, exercise, and expression.

We begin to understand the inner self only when we start to understand who we are, where we have come from, our purpose in choosing this life, and how to achieve that purpose.

In varying ways, we are all searching, but generally the search is for something external. We need to realize that the answers lie within, for as thinking, sensitive people, we need more answers to life than religion, politics, or science have so far delivered.

We need guidance, not promises; examples, not theories. And this is what I hope to deliver in the pages that follow.

This book is offered to the keen student of life who, perhaps unconsciously, has been searching for the answers to life's many unsolved enigmas. You will discover who you really are and how you can further improve and understand your life. Numerology can also help you to relate better to other people, become more emotionally and financially secure, maintain good health, and live a thoroughly loving life.

The Science of Numbers, as originally taught by Pythagoras, is about to be revealed. Are you prepared for an exciting journey... a journey that will take you to the heart of your inner self?

DAY 1

Understanding Numbers and the Three Aspects of Self

To the material scientist, numbers are merely symbols of comparative quantity. To the metaphysical scientist, or numerologist, numbers assume a more profound significance. They represent aspects of what it is to be human. Today we are going to examine the metaphysical meanings of numbers and explore the three-fold nature of human beings.

To truly understand numerology, we must first learn a little of Pythagoras, the Greek mathematician and philosopher who explored the mystery of numbers.

Pythagoras Reveals the Wonder of Numbers

Born in 608 B.C., Pythagoras sought to free the human mind from political and religious confinement. The essence of his teachings was enshrined in the axiom: "Know thyself, then thou shalt know the universe and God."

Pythagoras founded his own university at Crotona, a Greek colony in southern Italy, around 532 B.C. Admission was open to all who sincerely sought to learn.

The major course taught was in self-development, and was provided in a three-part curriculum. The primary component was known as "Preparation." It consisted of intensive training in the "ten mathematical disciplines," designed to provide the student with "empire over the self."

The second trimester was called "Purification." Its essence was the understanding of life, its purpose, and how to work in harmony with that purpose, as taught through the "Science of Numbers," more commonly known today as numerology.

In the final trimester, students were taught the concept of "Perfection." Perfection embraced the integration of the physical, mental, and spiritual components of each person and of life.

Metaphysical Meanings

Let us start with the essential metaphysical meanings of the numbers as based on the original meanings taught 2,500 years ago by Pythagoras.

- **ONE** is the first physical number. As the only absolute number, it is the symbol of divine expression. It is the key to verbal self-expression and the expression of the ego as a microcosm of the divine (the macrocosm). It is the key to our communication skills.

- **TWO** is the first spiritual (feeling) number. It represents the duality of humans and symbolizes the gateway to our sensitivities, as well as our need to be part of a pair. It is the number of intuition.

- **THREE** is the first mind (thinking) number. It is the gateway to the conscious mind and to rational understanding, the focus of left-brain activity, the key to memory. The number 3 is symbolized by the triangle, representing the connection of mind, soul, and body.

- **FOUR** is the number at the center of the Physical (doing) Plane, the key to orderliness, practicality, and organizing. It is symbolized by the square, the basis of all practical construction.

- **FIVE** is the center of the Soul (feeling) Plane and the very center of the total Birth Chart. It is the spiritual number representing love and freedom of expression.

- **SIX** is the center of the Mind (thinking) Plane, where it represents creativity and the integration of the left and right lobes of the brain. It also represents destruction. This is "negative" creativity, expressed as worry, stress, anxiety, and depression.

- **SEVEN** is the symbol of the temple, the human body and its seven chakras or power centers. It is the teaching learning number, the number of practical philosophical experience.

- **EIGHT** is the most active spiritual number. It is the number of wisdom expressed intuitively through loving action. It brings independence into focus.

- **NINE** is the three-fold number at the action end of the Mind Plane. As mind in action, it represents ambition (the physical aspect), responsibility (the thinking aspect) and idealism (the spiritual aspect), and so combines the attributes of each of the previous numbers.

- **ZERO** is a symbol rather than a number. The 0 is present in many birth dates and has an important symbolic significance. Philosophically and mathematically, it represents nothing (as the numerator) and everything (as the denominator), the two infinite ends of the finite, neither of which is physically attainable. Thus, it is a totally mystical symbol, indicative of the degree of spiritual mysticism inherent (but rarely developed) in the individual.

The Three Levels of Self

To penetrate the deeper level of human awareness, it's important to understand the nature of human beings, and how our "three selves" are intimately connected.

Three terms are used to succinctly and simply describe our three selves: Basic Self, Conscious Self, and High Self. Let me explain each in turn.

Basic Self

The primary level of human expression is through the body. Expression of the five physical senses (seeing, hearing, touching, tasting, and smelling) constitutes the primary functions of Basic Self, together with talking, laughing, crying, and all other physical activities.

Insecurity, sensation-seeking, the desire for control, or just blatant exhibitionism are the expressions of Basic Self. It is the body in self-defense; it is instinctive behavior. Basic Self people are ego-motivated, and their wants often supersede their needs. They are noticeably left-brain motivated.

Basic Self is vital to balanced expression while in the physical body. In fact, it is the body in action when total integration with the other two "selves" is present. Otherwise, it is the body in "reaction."

As we learn to control Basic Self, it becomes our faithful physical servant. Ego is then motivated by compassion and wisdom, our physical lives become organized, and we become more patient with ourselves and others. We evolve from the victim to the victor.

Basic Self in its fullness is the positive connection of the three numbers of the Physical Plane: 1, 4, and 7.

Conscious Self

The home of our thoughts and attitudes, Conscious Self can also be the seat of our joy and sadness. It is the domain of memory, creativity, and idealism.

Conscious Self is the bridge between Basic Self and High Self, integrating our reactive and instinctive aspects with our spiritual values. It is the connection between the left and right lobes of our brain.

When it chooses to be negative, Conscious Self becomes "unconscious self." It becomes deceitful, reactive, evasive, and stress-ridden, and adopts the role of victim.

However, if we allow it to fulfill its ultimate purpose, Conscious Self is the great appraiser. Conscious Self helps us to interpret intuition, love, and wisdom. It's the place where knowledge, compassion, and wisdom are translated into positive action.

Conscious Self is anchored in the memory; it links past knowledge with present experience to create a repository of information. When used positively, this repository becomes the basis of our confidence and self-esteem, and expands to embrace enhanced creativity and, even further, intelligent idealism.

The three numbers of the Mind Plane are 3, 6, and 9, and they unite to empower Conscious Self.

High Self

Including our moral virtues, philosophical ideas, and spiritual values, High Self is the essence of sensitivity and feeling, the aspect of our being that recognizes and determines our needs. It expresses itself as intuition, love, and wisdom. It is our highest form of expression, the God within. Action through High Self is largely right-brained: creative, spiritual, and compassionate.

True love is a function of High Self. Love has a depth that permeates every facet of positive human expression. It enjoys expression through the emotions, but it is not governed by them.

High Self is best facilitated through the development of our intuition, which leads to personal freedom, compassion, and a profound depth of wisdom.

In numerology, High Self is represented as the Soul or Feeling Plane, comprising the numbers 2, 5, and 8. The new millennium (with every birth date at least including a 2) will continue to see a more genuine spirituality manifested in human affairs.

DAY 2

Devising Your Birth Chart

When we want to open a locked door, we need the key. For most people, the inner self is behind a locked door, for rarely do they discover who they really are or develop their ultimate potential. The key to discovering the inner self through numerology is the Birth Chart. Today you are going to learn how to set up your own Birth Chart.

The primary purpose of the Birth Chart is to reveal at a glance the overall formula or pattern of our strengths and weaknesses. Each different birth date results in a different Birth Chart— there are almost endless variations, but the construction is always the same.

Handed down from teacher to teacher over the centuries in its pure, uncorrupted form, let me introduce you to the noble simplicity of the Pythagorean Birth Chart.

Step 1

Convert your birth date to its full numerical equivalent. For example, if you were born January 21, 1963, you would convert it to 1/21/1963. (Always remember to include the full year.)

Step 2

The Birth Chart is constructed of four short, straight lines: two drawn horizontally, two vertically. The vertical lines intersect the horizontal lines like a noughts-and-crosses layout.

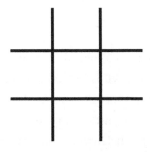

This empty Birth Chart is symbolic of a baby as yet unborn.

Step 3

Each of the nine spaces is the permanent home for each of the nine numbers. Whenever a number appears in a birth date, it must always be placed in its own space, nowhere else. If numbers are absent from the birth date, the corresponding spaces of the Birth Chart remain empty.

If all numbers were present in the birth date, the completed Birth Chart would appear as fully balanced:

3	6	9
2	5	8
1	4	7

This reveals no missing numbers; it further reveals an impossibility. The most numbers we can have in our birth date is eight, of which the numbers 1, 2, or 3 must be repeated. The maximum number of spaces that can be filled in a Birth Chart is seven, such as when a person has a birth date of 5/27/1983.

3		9
2	5	8
1		7

How we handle the Birth Chart when any number in the birth date is repeated is exactly the same as the previous example. For example, take the birth dates 11/11/1999 and 2/20/2000. The two Birth Charts would appear as:

11/11/1999   2/20/2000

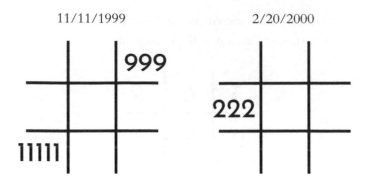

Obviously, the maximum number of empty spaces on a Birth Chart for the 20th century is seven, while for the 21st century it is eight. A further important aspect is the absence of 0 from any Birth Chart. Its repeated presence in a birth date reduces the prevalence of Birth Chart numbers, and in turn reveals vital growth needs as in the second example.

To construct your own Birth Chart, simply draw a naked Birth Chart and fill in the spaces with your birth date numbers.

Step 4

With your Birth Chart now constructed, you have your basic individuality formula in place. We are now ready to analyze its many and various aspects. But first we need to observe the overall Birth Chart in its entirety, as a key to unlocking vital secrets of the inner self.

We must recognize the three Selves as expressed on the three Planes that comprise the Birth Chart.

MIND PLANE (mental thinking)	**3**	**6**	**9**	CONSCIOUS SELF
SOUL PLANE (spiritual, feeling)	**2**	**5**	**8**	HIGH SELF
BASIC SELF (practical, doing)	**1**	**4**	**7**	PHYSICAL PLANE

Here we see the balanced Birth Chart with its three Planes and their meanings. The degree of concentration of numbers on each Plane gives a general indication of which Self is most fluently expressed.

This knowledge is extremely beneficial in human relationships, for it reveals the level of communication most favored by each person. The following example clearly illustrates this important aspect of numerology:

Shirley Maclaine, born 4/24/1934

3		**9**
2		
1	**444**	

In spite of her 1980s lapse into New Age spirituality, Shirley's Birth Chart formula clearly reveals her Soul Plane to be her weakest. Her dominant strength appears in her Physical Plane with her compounded 4's. Little wonder she was so easily enticed back to work in the entertainment industry. This is not to say that she has deserted the spiritual, for it is clear that she needs to develop this undernourished aspect of herself, so it depends whether she wishes to develop this side of herself.

The Meaning of Each Plane

Mind Plane: This represents the human head and is symbolically found on the top line of the Birth Chart. It embraces memory, thinking, analyzing, rationalizing, imagining, creating, responsibility, ambition, and idealism.

Soul Plane: This represents the human heart and is symbolically found in the center of the Birth Chart, from where it governs sensitivity. It also embraces intuition, love, freedom, positive emotions, artistic expression, spiritual independence, and wisdom.

Physical Plane: This represents human activity and is symbolically found at the base of the Birth Chart. It embraces verbal expression, motivation, body language, organization, patience, materialism, and learning through sacrifice.

DAY 3

The Numbers on Your Birth Chart

Today, and over the next several days, we are going to take a close look at the numbers that appear on Birth Charts. We begin with an overview of the numbers.

Number 1

Located at the entrance to the Physical Plane, the number 1 refers to the expression of the physical body in terms of its relationship to the outside world. It is usually a reliable indication of the extent to which a person reacts to other people and circumstances. It indicates the degree of personal self-control—or its lack. This number is the foundation of the personality, for it represents the ego and how it is expressed or suppressed.

Number 2

Found at the gateway to the Soul Plane, 2 is the key to intuition, sensitivity, and feeling. After the numbers 1 and 9, 2 is the most common found in birth dates of the 20th century, and is the most common number of the 21st century. To possess a 2 on your Birth Chart is a blessing, for it provides you with a valuable guide to the degree of your sensitivity and intuition. As those born in the 21st century grow to maturity and take increased responsibility in human affairs, the 20th century's egocentricity and ambition will give way to an intuitive sensitivity to world affairs. Meanwhile, do not assume that birth dates without a number 2 indicate a total absence of intuition and sensitivity. Rather, this simply suggests that these traits need to be developed.

Number 3

Not only is this the gateway number to the Mind Plane, but it is also the most essential of the mind numbers for it governs memory. The single number 3 indicates the most desirable strength both for itself and to assist balanced power elsewhere in the Birth Chart.

Absence of the number 3 on the Birth Chart does not imply mental weakness unless the person succumbs to laziness and/ or indifference. Generally, it indicates that the person needs to exert greater effort in the mental spheres.

Number 4

Symbolically, the 4 represents containment and regularity as depicted by the square. It is a practical and material number, located squarely in the center of the Physical Plane of the Birth Chart. People with this number are generally tidy and meticulous, practical and organized. Birth Charts without a 4 indicate a degree of impatience in the person, but how impatient they are depends significantly upon other numerological factors, such as the Ruling Number (see Day 9) and Day Number (see Day 14). Such an impatient disposition can be largely overcome by conscious attention to detail and by care and concern for other people's needs.

Number 5

The unique position of this number in the center of the Birth Chart demands special attention, for it governs the intensity of human feelings. As the second number on the Soul (Feeling) Plane, 5 is the numerological equivalent of the heart chakra, for it symbolizes love and freedom of expression, emotionally and artistically.

It is the only number on the Birth Chart to have direct contact with every other number. Its other unique factor is its containment, being completely boxed in and surrounded, whereas each of the other eight numbers is open to the universe. At first glance, this might appear a paradox for the number that represents freedom, but it actually indicates how freedom must be attained—by dismantling barriers.

Number 6

Located in the center of the Mind Plane, the number 6 represents human creativity as well as its opposite, destruction. The choice is always ours as to whether we embrace the positive or negative aspects of a number, but from 6 through to 9, the divergence between the two aspects becomes more pronounced. Because we are microscopic aspects of the macrocosmic power of the Creator, the same creativity is inherent within us all. The 6 provides the creative link between the 3 of memory and analysis (left brain) and the 9 of responsible idealism (right brain); it facilitates the smooth and constructive working of the Mind Plane.

The number 6 also brings the will into harmony with the mind. This is achieved with the support of the practical love of the 4 and the love of the 5 underpinning it.

Birth Charts with no number 6 indicate the need for the person to consciously develop their creative faculties through the powers of their existing numbers.

Number 7

As the highest number of the Physical Plane, 7 represents a special function of human life. It indicates the amount of learning one must amass, generally through the personal experience of sacrifice. Its deeper, philosophical significance lies in two domains: physically, 7 represents practical activity as the means for consummate learning and teaching; spiritually, 7 is the "temple" number, the repository of philosophy, truth, and wisdom. This further indicates the need to detach from worldly possessions in order to integrate body and soul.

Lack of a 7 on the Birth Chart reveals that either the person has evolved through that form of sacrifice in recent past lives or the person does not have the necessary philosophical understanding of sacrifice and has to put practical effort into achieving it.

Number 8

As the most active number of the Soul Plane, 8 exerts a dual influence. Spiritually, it is the number of wisdom; physically, it is the number of active independence. Symbolically, 8 appears as the double 4, the double square, one atop the other. This elevates some of the organizational and practical aspects of the 4 onto the higher plane of expression, revealing the close affinity between the 4 and 8, though they are on totally different planes.

Birth Charts without an 8 indicate that those people have to deliberately apply themselves to achieve the desirable level of wisdom and independence that makes life more fulfilling and rewarding.

Number 9

A most powerful number, the Romans regarded 9 as the war number, symbolizing the planet Mars. We know it to be a number of war *and* prosperity, but so much depends on how it is used. As the number symbolizing mental activity, 9 is also representative of the right lobe of our brain and its power of idealism, its spiritual component.

Its physical counterpart manifests as ambition, which caused so much international strife and confusion in the world in the 20th century. From the beginning of this century, more people have been born without a 9 on their Birth Chart. At the same time, everyone will have at least one 2, thereby greatly transferring the emphasis from the Mind to the Soul Plane. In summary, more people will have deep feelings and there will be less egocentric ambitiousness. However, this will not become significantly apparent until closer to the middle of this century, when those born at its beginning will be mature and responsible enough to take the reins of decision-making.

DAY 4

Interpreting Your Birth Chart: Single Numbers

Today we continue to explore the numbers on Birth Charts with an examination of those that appear singly.

One 1

Birth dates with a single 1 belong to people who have difficulty in verbal self-expression. This is not to imply they cannot speak well; rather, it indicates the difficulty they have in expressing their inner feelings. Until they develop self-mastery—a product of maturity and understanding—self-expression will not come easily to them.

At times, they will intentionally say the opposite of what they mean as a form of aggressive defense, as a self-protection mechanism. This invariably compounds the initial problem.

They must learn to think before they speak and can do so by taking command of their responses rather than reacting, as the spoken word is often impossible to retract and hurt feelings are difficult to mend.

One 2

Birth Charts with a single 2 indicate a sound, basic level of intuition—but not always enough in this highly competitive world, especially for men.

A single 2 provides a valuable foundation for developing balanced sensitivity. Women possess a "de facto" 2 on their Birth Chart, for their very natures are more sensitive and intuitive than those of men. Thus, with a single 2 on their Birth Chart, women are blessed with the equivalent of the balanced double 2, whereas men have to diligently practice developing balanced sensitivity.

In general, people with one 2 on their Birth Chart find that they need time to relax in nature away from the intensity of competitive living. An individual's Ruling Number (see Day 9) is the most reliable guide for how to do this.

One 3

As the anchor of memory, the single 3 on the Birth Chart provides a natural quality that will capably support people with it throughout life. This 3 makes it easy for them to maintain alert mental activity.

The power of the 3 is a great natural aid to the young. It will assist them with their education, formally and informally. They will maintain an active interest in life and the environment.

As mental strength and agility are vital foundations for the cultivation of a balanced and optimistic understanding of life, these people generally have happy dispositions and can readily apply themselves successfully to most tasks. They usually possess an above-average level of self-confidence, which also contributes to their success in life.

One 4

These are active people who express a natural identity with the practical, including organizational, technical, financial, and/or physical involvements (gardening, manual arts, building, and so on).

Preferring to work with concrete rather than theoretical concepts, these people become impatient with unwarranted delays and procrastination, as they want to get on with the task at hand.

Too much emphasis on the physical can make them somewhat materialistic. This is a negative aspect of the 4, and its intention is to teach them to use their natural patience to avoid extreme materialism, best achieved through the development of care and compassion for others.

One 5

With the single 5 in the center of the Birth Chart, the best chance of achieving a balanced personality becomes available. It is also the only number that ensures that none of the corner numbers takes on their isolated qualities (see Day 8). In particular, the single 5 greatly assists the individual in achieving emotional control, for it ensures that their sensitivity to life develops as a reliable intuitive guide. This allows them to become more adept at choosing suitable courses of action, rather than responding to situations through thoughtless reaction.

As a valuable protection to sensitivity, the single 5 strengthens fortitude and compassion, thereby creating strength of character. It also provides the power of love and freedom that enhances all other forms of expression. The single 5 assists the individual in understanding their own feelings and so encourages a deep appreciation for the feelings of others.

One 6

The number of creativity, 6 finds its most common expression in the deep love of the home. However, its more personal expression can be found in the artistic fields, such as pottery, painting, composing, acting, and similar disciplines.

People with one 6 have a strong focus on domestic responsibility, which tends to mask the true role of the 6—creative expression. However, as these people become more aware and mature, they will find that domestic satisfaction alone leaves much to be desired. It is then that they will exert their strength of will to bring more personal creativity into their lives—or they will continue to wonder why they are not receiving sufficient fulfillment from their endeavors. As they "discover" the arts and especially the creative power of music, their lives will blossom amazingly.

One 7

As part of the vital learning process of life, sacrifices in matters of health, love, money, or possessions will be encountered when this number appears on the Birth Chart. This is only intended as part of the soul's unfolding. The sufferers often bemoan the sacrifices, as they do not understand the vital role of "giving up to acquire."

If we are to fulfill our purpose here on Earth, we must ensure that our health is properly nourished. In love, all too often we confuse desire with unconditional love. Remember, we can never lose if we practice unconditional love, but we rarely retain love when we associate it with emotional demands and expectations.

One 8

These people are most methodical and meticulous when living positively. On the other hand, apathy and instability prevail when they exist negatively.

Tidiness, with considerable attention to detail and a feel for efficiency, is natural to these people. These are the aspects of practical wisdom that underlie their development. However, if these people choose the negative path, they become emotionally unstable, reactive, and restless, resulting in frequent changes in home, career, or relationships.

One 9

Ambition, responsibility, and idealism—these are the three major qualities of the 9. This power has been at the foundation of humanity's driving force for the past century, responsible for our drive to find out more about life and to control it more. Not that it appears to have succeeded very well. Though we know infinitely more about our environment and what it is to be human than we did at the beginning of the 20th century, we also have more environmental degradation, human sickness, and suffering, and extensive famine and poverty than at any time in the past two centuries. What went wrong? Could it be that too much focus was put on ambition and not enough on responsibility and idealism?

DAY 5

Interpreting Your Birth Chart: Two of the Same Number

Today we consider the meaning of having two of the same number on your Birth Chart.

Two 1's

Blessed with the gift of balanced self-expression, people with two 1's are the most fortunate people. It is a valuable Birth Chart characteristic that should be used wisely—never abuse it for manipulative purposes.

The person with two 1's is often able to see both sides of a situation or argument, and it is not uncommon for them to take the other side midway through a discussion if it should suddenly appear more valid. This makes for an extremely broad understanding of situations and people.

Many successful politicians and other public figures are found to have two 1's. It tends to heighten humanitarian awareness and expression.

Two 2's

The balance of the second 2 on the Birth Chart is a great advantage, providing the ideal quality for the easy development of intuitive sensitivity. An innate perception endows these people with an intelligence that is above average, based on an acute natural ability to read and understand people and circumstances. They possess a great gift when it comes to first impressions, being able to form almost instant, accurate opinions of people and concepts.

The balanced intuitive sensitivity of these people tends to draw them to become involved in many aspects of human affairs. They generally do so with significant success, but need to guard against becoming too available for too many worthy causes, which could be detrimental to their personal happiness. As always, balance is the key to their success.

Two 3's

With increased mental alertness come a more active imagination and increased literary ability. Such power has to be carefully disciplined to avoid what might become antisocial behavior if allowed to run riot.

To facilitate self-discipline, the practice of meditation is valuable, together with memory training and the development of intuition. Without constructive thought processes the active brain of the two 3's will place too much emphasis on imagination, to the detriment of objective planning, investigation, and positive comprehension.

Most people with two 3's on their Birth Charts have significant writing ability, though they rarely realize this without outside help. They need to be encouraged to put their thoughts and imaginings on paper, for this will stimulate free-flowing literary expression. In turn, such expression will help these people channel this quality, and perhaps readily turn it into a lucrative source of income.

Two 4's

The double 4 can lead to an unbalanced outlook that relates everything to the physical and material. The powerful utilitarian aspect of these people must seek balanced expression between the physical, mental, and spiritual, allowing them to identify and be in harmony with their thoughts and feelings.

The more 4's on the Birth Chart, the greater the need for balance and care in choosing friends. They should especially endeavor to steer clear of hard-drinking, heavy-smoking types, for they require far more sensitivity from friends and colleagues if they are to develop balance in their lives. These people will benefit from the company of others who enjoy the aesthetic and cultural qualities of life.

Two 5's

People with this concentration of 5's are frequently recognized for their driving intensity. Intensified determination gives them an air of great confidence and self-assurance, which can often be more wishful than factual. As they mature, this self-assurance diminishes to mere bravado, and they find it difficult to cope with the troubles that emerge in their lives.

Their drive and enthusiasm can at times become overbearing and cause misunderstandings. So intense are they in the expression of their attitudes that they often create emotional turmoil and develop ulcers and health problems in the solar plexus area, as well as indigestion.

Special care should be taken by these people to exercise emotional control, or they could easily become dependent on drugs or sex for the relief and/or release of pent-up emotional energy.

Two 6's

The double 6 can be either a mighty challenge or a heavy handicap. How the individual handles it depends on many factors, such as their Ruling Number (see Day 9) and environmental factors, particularly the early influence of their parents.

With less-aware people, the negative aspects will be initially inclined to prevail. These produce worry, anxiety, stress, and irritability, particularly around the home and workplace. They must be guided, never pushed or threatened. Love and appreciation are vital to them, acting as a balm to their alert nervous systems.

These people require much more rest than most, for they use much nervous energy. They must learn to meditate before going to bed to ensure that their sleep is deeply restful. When possible, and if desired, they should take the time for an afternoon siesta.

Two 7's

Two 7's indicates the intensity of the lessons that need to be undertaken through sacrifice in two of the three basic areas of life: health, love, or money and possessions. The intensity of the experience is intended to focus the individual upon the deeper philosophical understanding of life. This stimulates our interest in the metaphysical, which develops our powers for healing, guidance, and compassion.

When not living positively, these people fail to develop that indispensable philosophical understanding of life, of which they are so capable. Instead, they constantly complain about loss, blame others for their problems, and accuse life of being grossly unfair. They become grumpy, pitiful individuals that most people prefer to avoid.

Two 8's

The sharpened power of assessment of the two 8's on the Birth Chart can be either extremely beneficial or highly unsettling, depending on how positive the individual is. In matters demanding special attention to detail, these people can excel. But they must be aware that their perceptiveness does not allow them to become dictatorial from overconfidence. This would give rise to inward emotional conflict, resulting in instability and extreme restlessness.

Their search for truth and wisdom can stimulate such restlessness, but in a positive manner. It inspires them to travel, which is a wonderful source of knowledge and wisdom. If they do not travel when they are young, deep frustration can develop, exacerbating their irritability. This can lead to a feeling of confinement, and only when travel opportunities are fulfilled do they eventually find peace of mind.

Two 9's

An intensity of idealism and zeal, coupled with serious thought, characterizes these people. They often express such an overzealous idealism that it becomes impractical to implement. They must be careful to maintain a sound level of practicality to balance the idealism.

The inclination to become critical of others with a lower level of idealism must be guarded against and overcome if they are to find happiness. Yet these people are deep thinkers, and at the heart of all they do, they wish to be helpful. It just needs to be clearly expressed and they must not expect it to be taken for granted.

DAY 6

Interpreting Your Birth Chart: Three of the Same Number

Today we delve into the meaning of having three of the same number on your Birth Chart.

Three 1's

There are two distinctly different types of expression here. The most frequently encountered is the talkative type, the chatterbox who is invariably bright and interesting. They generally find life enjoyable and seek to share that enjoyment with others.

The second group comprises a minority, who also have no numbers on the Soul Plane. They are generally quiet, introspective, and occasionally shy, especially with strangers. However, they do tend to become perky and talkative in friendly company. These people find they can express themselves better through writing, where their thoughts flow more freely, uninhibited by their acute sensitivity.

Three 2's

Three 2's on a Birth Chart indicates a hypersensitivity that can become quite an emotional load to carry for some people. It indicates that the person is highly attuned to others' feelings, resulting in an inclination to become involved in other people's problems.

Many people with three 2's work in the entertainment field, where they achieve remarkable success, sensitively portraying other characters. However, difficulty in expressing deep personal feelings also arises from such sensitivity, leading to hurt. They then tend to become defensive and impulsively say hurtful things.

How children with three 2's cope with life will depend largely on their parents, who need to help their children achieve a solid basis of self-confidence, in line with the path indicated by the child's Ruling Number (see Day 9).

Three 3's

With great emphasis on mental activity and expression, people with three 3's often lose contact with reality, resulting in isolation and loneliness. Their fertile imagination is so intent on thinking ahead and conceiving weird scenarios that they often find it difficult to focus on the present and to relate to other people.

With such an overbalance, these people find trust difficult to accept, are rarely relaxed, and may become addicted to stress-relieving drugs. They are sometimes so absorbed in their mental adventures that they become oblivious to everything around them. Their introversion exacerbates their distrust of other people, often leading to argumentativeness.

These people need patient, understanding, and caring assistance and the best way to provide this is to encourage them to focus on the present moment. They need to be taught practicality through the conscious application of their hands and hearts to manual activity of an artistic nature.

Three 4's

All the aspects of the double 4 prevail here, only with greater intensity, for these people experience even greater difficulty rising above the physical, and are so often drawn back by materialism. Those who recognize this pull to materialism must employ great effort of will and be receptive to dedicated, caring guidance.

Many people with this aspect feel the pull toward hard, manual work and persist with it to the point of exhaustion, not realizing that their lesson is the mastery of it, rather than enslavement to it. Only through such mastery do they acquire the desirable balance between the physical, mental, and spiritual expression. They must guard against relating everything to the physical and going overboard about such concerns as neatness.

People with three or four 4's have a tendency toward weak lower limbs, for they place a lot of emphasis on the legs. They should take exceptional care of their knees, ankles, and feet.

Three 5's

Points made for the double 5 (see Day 5) are even more intensified when a person has three 5's on their Birth Chart. Such emotional intensity as this can be very difficult for many people to handle. Fortunately, few are born with this extreme intensity of drive and feeling.

Very special and careful training in self-discipline has to be a vital part of the early lives of these people. This places unique responsibility on the parents, who often feel lost in failing to understand their complex child. Parents should not despair; as their love and understanding wins through, they will realize how much they have learned from the experience.

Thinking before speaking or acting will enable the influence of wisdom to prevail and will avoid offending the sensitivity of such intense people.

Three 6's

With three 6's on the Birth Chart comes greater worry concerning the home, worry that is of the individual's own making. Women with three 6's suffer more, for they usually do not seek to be involved in anything outside the home.

Many people with this combination rarely realize its positive potential for brilliant creativity. Instead, they turn it inward, and it becomes a tornado of disturbed emotions. They secretly fear their children growing up and leaving home, creating an unhealthy possessiveness that ultimately drives the children away earlier than might have otherwise occurred.

Special care must be taken to achieve balance in their lives. Adequate rest, creative expression, and care with diet will provide the appropriate corrective measures.

Three 7's

Superficially, three 7's in a Birth Chart appears to result in sad lives brought about by heavy losses in health, love, and money. But the sadness is often more unsettling to the close associate than it is to the sufferer who, with such a depth of philosophical understanding, recognizes the purpose behind the events.

Such loss tests these people's fortitude and compassion, endowing them with enormous strength of character. This can make for a truly remarkable person, a valuable friend whose outlook grows with maturity, displaying almost infinite depths of wisdom. Such is only the case with those people with three 7's who recognize opportunity in every challenge.

For those negative souls who prefer to languish and rely on sympathy to justify their existence, the tendency toward depression and anti-social behavior loses them many friends and further exacerbates their problems.

Three 8's

The acute restlessness induced by the negative aspect of three 8's is more frequently met than its opposite. To feel that life is pointless and frustrating is to be a victim of the most extreme pessimism. So these people need considerable love and guidance to encourage them to adopt a largely positive outlook on life.

For the positive person with three 8's, great wisdom and a glorious feeling of independence underpins their daily living. Even though they prefer to be on the go, they have an inner stability and a joyousness that wins them many friends.

Three 9's

The exceptional power of idealism and ambition of the three 9's is extremely difficult to handle and can at times produce mental imbalance. This problem can be avoided by recognizing the three 9's in the Birth Charts of children and training them to balance their expression more evenly over the three Planes.

It is not uncommon for these people, when acting negatively, to allow small things to become exaggerated out of all proportion. This often results in outbursts of temper, leading to loss of emotional control, even to the extent of threatening mental balance.

The vital lesson here is to look at all things objectively and in proportion to their real value. This will help dissolve their judgment and permit the acceptance of small deviations from their rigid idealism.

DAY 7

Interpreting Your Birth Chart: Four of the Same Number

Today we examine the meaning of having four of the same number on your Birth Chart.

Four 1's

People with four 1's experience difficulty with verbal expression and are therefore often misunderstood. But life soon teaches them to hide emotional turmoil with a smile, though they tend to suffer inwardly unless they learn to release such emotions.

Highly egocentric, these people identify with those for whom they share deep feelings. For their personal happiness and that of the people close to them, it is important for people with four 1's to take command of their emotions. As they relax more and improve in self-confidence, they will feel less inhibited and become freer to express, rather than suppress, their inner feelings.

Four 2's

Such a high level of impressionability has to be carefully and continuously disciplined or it will easily erupt into severe misrepresentations, invariably accompanied by bad temper, sarcasm, and spite. These people are often extremely impatient. Their intuition becomes unreliable as they misinterpret so much, and they invariably overreact and become quite volatile and emotionally unbalanced.

Extreme patience and understanding needs to be shown by family and friends. The lives of people with four 2's are often very lonely, and many turn to drugs, alcohol, and other substances. They can avoid emotional isolation if they undergo appropriate counseling. They need to learn to firmly apply self-control when it comes to emotional expression, to relax and meditate as needed, and to flow with the movement of life.

Four 3's

This unusual amount of 3's can only occur during one month of any century—it last transpired on 3/31/1933 and will not occur again until 3/3/2033.

The excessive imagination and mental hyperactivity of these people can bring them to the point of intense fear, worry, and confusion. They have little or no regard for physical concerns, with a terribly impractical outlook in general.

As understanding them demands so much of others, they rarely have close friends. Yet that is exactly what they need, most especially someone who will help direct their attention toward more practical concerns. They need to be encouraged and taught practical activities, such as dressmaking, hairdressing, landscaping, interior decorating, and writing. They must become involved in the "doing" side of life.

Four 4's

This is another extremely rare occurrence; it last happened on 4/24/1944 and will next occur on 4/4/2044.

Due to the strong pull of the physical, extreme care in all activities must be taken, and there exists a critical weakness in their lower limbs.

All the advice and help suggested for those with three 4's (see Day 6) applies even more when four 4's appear on the Birth Chart. Extreme patience is demanded with these people; as they are so highly skeptical of metaphysical concepts, you can easily become bored with their extreme pragmatism.

Four 5's

This occurs as rarely as the four 3's and 4's, fortunately. The last person with four 5's was born on 5/25/1955, and the next birth will not occur until 5/5/2055.

The overwhelming intensity of feeling and sensitivity within the solar plexus of these people means they are generally in a state of advanced stress. Life has the habit of inflicting "accidents" upon us to either slow us down or to turn us around if we have digressed from the Path. But if we do not reassess our situation, we may find more intense "accidents" strewn along our path. This is typical of person with four 5's.

Life for these people can be very difficult to understand if they do not permit wise guidance to direct them.

Four 6's

Four 6's on a Birth Chart only occurs thrice a century, the last being 6/26/1966, which at least had the additional numbers 1, 2, and 9 on the Birth Chart to provide some relief. But the next birth date with four 6's occurs on 6/26/2066, and only provides two 2's as additional help, thereby focusing even more strongly on the heavy burden of the four 6's.

While four 6's indicates exceptional creative potential, the negative aspect, as stimulated by the emotions, is ready to dominate. As such, these people are likely to become pathetic worriers, sabotaging their health and friendships because of endless complaining. This is, of course, unless their parents have recognized this tendency and have lovingly and patiently guided their child's creative potential. The positive expression of the four 6's can be easily achieved with unconditional love.

Four 7's

During July 1977, I felt deep compassion for the infants born on the 7th, 17th and 27th, as well as the parents who had no idea of the problems they would face with such children. Fortunately, no more souls will incarnate with four 7's until 7/7/2077.

To both the children and the parents of children with four 7's, exceedingly careful help is necessary, else all will feel the burden of such compounded sacrifice. Yet, once understood, it can be an exciting learning experience. A change in attitude is necessary to see the half-full rather than the half-empty glass.

The heightened philosophical understanding that attends such a life provides wonderful potential for rapid growth in spiritual consciousness. But certain basic training is necessary in the form of essential personal disciplines by which the person learns to gain "empire over the self," as Pythagoras so eloquently phrased it.

Four 8's

The last person to be born with four 8's was on 8/28/1988, and the next such birth will not occur until 8/8/2088.

They are extremely hyperactive, restless people. As infants and children, they should never be forced to sit and watch television or told to "sit still," for this will only lead to excessive frustration and, ultimately, quite irrational behavior from pent-up emotions. They should be taught to develop a sound sense of direction and be taken places as often as possible until they are old enough to travel on their own.

Four 9's

From time to time, we come across people born with four 9's on their Birth Chart. Though they comprise only a small fraction of the population, they invariably need help. Among them we generally find two distinct types.

The most common are those who live in a dream world of unreality. They have often dropped out of society because they could not come to grips with what didn't match their idealism. Some appear to be "normal" and conforming until, from time to time, they can take it no more and either go far away or lock themselves in their homes for days or months on end. But these are quite harmless people who simply deny that anything is wrong and do not respond well to guidance.

The other type are those who adopt an aggressive, belligerent attitude and appear to take pleasure in belittling others. These can be dangerous and should receive wise counseling before they become irreversibly lonely or do harm to themselves or someone else in a fit of rage.

DAY 8

Interpreting Your Birth Chart: Five or More of the Same Number and Isolated Numbers

Today we complete our look at the Birth Chart by considering the meaning of five or more of the same number and the significance of isolated numbers.

Five or more 1's

With five, six, or seven 1's on the Birth Chart, ego suppression is created to counteract the basic difficulty with verbal expression. Young people with these numbers can indeed be sad as they are often misunderstood. This creates aloofness, which leads in turn to increasing loneliness. They can become somewhat obsessive about their appearance, secretly adoring looking at themselves. Such egoism and deception can readily lead to mental imbalances.

Five 2's

This is an extremely rare occurrence; it last occurred on 12/2/2022. Individuals with five 2's are very likely to become totally reactive to their enormous sensitivity. They need devoted care and guidance, especially when young, and they will try another's patience to the ultimate.

Not only will more birth dates occur with five 2's in this millennium, but we will also find the occasional six 2's, the first born on 2/22/2022, and the rare seven 2's—on 2/22/2222 and 12/22/2222. In the last century, Birth Charts with five 2's also had at least a 1 and a 9, but in this millennium individuals with six or seven 2's will not have such a minor counterbalance, so will need special counseling and care when it comes to emotional expression.

Five 9's

A few infants with five 9's came into this world during September of the last year of the 20th century. Understanding them will be almost an impossibility without numerology, and helping them will be another even greater challenge.

Everything written about those with four 9's (see Day 7) applies to the five 9's, only with compounded significance. It is to be hoped that their parents are highly trained numerologists, for teaching them to be practical and compassionate will be the greatest challenge.

The Isolated Numbers

Many Birth Charts of the 20th century will have more empty spaces than full, a situation that becomes even more pronounced in the 21st century. This will often lead to the isolation of one or more of the corner numbers of the Birth Chart (1, 3, 7, and 9). These isolated numbers have special significance.

Isolated 1's

When the numbers 2, 5, and 4 are missing from a Birth Chart, the number 1 is isolated from all other numbers. As 1 is the number symbolizing the expression of the human ego, its isolation reveals why these people so often feel alone and misunderstood when they try to explain their feelings to others.

If their numbers are heavily concentrated on the Mind Plane, the person might be perceived as lazy or unreliable because so much going on in their head won't get translated into practical expression, or because they make commitments to do things that rarely get done.

Correction is easy. For every isolated number, the one quality missing that will integrate the Birth Chart and "de-isolate" each number is represented by the number 5 in the center. Generally, this implies the need for more love and compassion in their expression, and to show their positive emotions rather than bottle them up. When only the 1 is isolated, developing the intuition of the 2, so that the expression of the ego can be connected with the power of analysis (the 3) and practiced with the improved logic, patience and practicality of the 4, can also help.

Isolated 3's

When a single 3 or compounded 3's are alone in the upper left of the Birth Chart, with the numbers 2, 5, and 6 missing, the person has the "isolated 3" problem. This means that their strong mind potential can be easily diffused, for it is unconnected with the Physical Plane. This problem can be severely compounded when more than one 3 is isolated, for then the imagination can run riot.

Correction is similar to that employed for the isolated 1. The person needs to develop the power of the number 5 on their Birth Chart, followed by the development of their intuition through the power of the 2. This is similar to before, except that now verbal expression has to be linked to the mind's power so that it can be given vent.

The third force desirous of development is that of the creative 6. This will link the 3 with the 9 in every birth date of the 20th century. Learning to embrace creative outlets is the best way to develop the 6.

Isolated 7's

When one or more 7's occupy the lower right corner of the Birth Chart without a 4, 5, or 8 in contact with them, the sacrifices and lessons to be learned by the person are necessarily repeated. The experience of learning has to be translated to the mind for its lesson to be recognized and understood. But when the learning area is isolated from the Mind Plane, the same lessons have to be repeated until, by force of frequency, they become recognized.

To minimize the hurt or sacrifice, the person needs to develop the powers inherent in the numbers 4, 5, and 8. We have already covered the qualities of the 4 and 5 with the aforementioned isolated numbers, but now we see that the development of the 4 helps the isolated 7 to unify with the ego expression of the 1 to feel okay about asking for help or guidance.

To develop the power of the 8 on the Birth Chart, the isolated 7 must become wiser when it comes to applying practical intuition through loving action.

Isolated 9's

When the numbers 5, 6, and 8 are missing from the Birth Chart, and the person has one or more 9's (as do all in the 20th century), the individual either exhibits impractical idealism, unrequited ambition, or both. This generally depends on the number of 9's on the Birth Chart. If a single 9, it is usually the sign of unfulfilled ambition; if a double 9, impractical idealism; if three or four 9's, both may prevail.

From the corrective measures recommended for the other isolated numbers, the technique is easy to follow. In this case, the qualities of the 5, then the 6 and the 8 need to be inculcated into the person's expression. Of these, perhaps the 5 is the most important if the person does not have a 7 on their Birth Chart, for the 5 will link the 9's with expression through the ego of the number 1. If they have a 7 as well, then the powers of both numbers (5 and 8) should be developed for optimum connection between the ambition idealism of the 9 and the practical Physical Plane.

Remember, the power of your original Birth Chart is not as important as what you do to fill its empty spaces. Some of the most successful people in history have had some of the weakest and emptiest Birth Charts. Their success has only come about by developing the qualities they lacked initially to evolve toward perfection. That is the purpose of life.

DAY 9

Introducing
Ruling Numbers

So many people are led onto paths in life where their talents are not fully utilized, while others drift into jobs or activities that are as far removed from their most suitable pathways as bricklaying is for a ballerina. Yet if high school students were to be taught their Ruling Numbers, our subject for today and the next few days, they would be guided to a suitable job or to advanced study appropriate to their nature.

Fortunately, more and more people are realizing that to discover and follow their Path is the most rewarding thing they can do in life. Our strength and maturity emerge as we fulfill our primary purpose, as simply revealed by our Ruling Number.

Our Ruling Number is found by first adding together each individual number in our birth date. We then add those numbers together until we get a single-digit number. For example, if we take the birth date January 3, 1960 and rewrite it numerically as 1/3/1960, we get 20 as a result when we add all the numbers together: $1 + 3 + 1 + 9 + 6 + 0 = 20$. This total is then reduced to a single-digit number by simple adding $2 + 0$, which of course is 2. So, the Ruling Number of a person born on January 3, 1960 is shown as $1/3/1960 = 20/2$.

To clearly illustrate how each Ruling Number (11 in total) is obtained, the following birth dates have been used as examples:

- May 1, 1940: $5/1/1940 = 20/2$—Ruling Number of 2

- May 2, 1940: $5/2/1940 = 21/3$—Ruling Number of 3

- May 3, 1949: $5/3/1949 = 31/4$—Ruling Number of 4

- May 4, 1949: $5/4/1949 = 32/5$—Ruling Number of 5

- May 5, 1949: $5/5/1949 = 33/6$—Ruling Number of 6

- May 6, 1949: $5/6/1949 = 34/7$—Ruling Number of 7

- May 7, 1949: $5/7/1949 = 35/8$—Ruling Number of 8

- May 8, 1949: $5/8/1949 = 36/9$—Ruling Number of 9

- May 9, 1949: $5/9/1949 = 37/10$—Ruling Number of 10

- May 1, 1949: $5/1/1949 = 29/11$—Ruling Number of 11

- May 3, 1940: $5/3/1940 = 22/4$—Ruling Number of 22/4

Note that in Pythagorean numerology there is no Ruling Number 1. In the sixth century B.C., Pythagoras recognized 1 as the number symbolizing unity in the world and ego in humans. Thus, as every number contains the 1, in Pythagorean numerology we find the Ruling Number 10 instead of a Ruling Number 1. Therefore, birth dates totaling 19, 28, 37, or 46 become Ruling Number 10's.

The Ruling Number 10 is the first of the three compounded Ruling Numbers. The other two are Ruling Number 11 and Ruling Number 22/4. These two have a special metaphysical significance: the 11 is the highest spiritual number and the 22/4 (twenty-two four) is the double 11 underpinned by the practical 4, combining to form a truly masterful combination.

The 22 is recognized for its special significance in many metaphysical and scientific systems. It represents the highest card in the Major Arcana of the Tarot. In basic mathematics, the 22 represents the circle, for it is the lowest whole number to which the ratio of the circumference with the diameter of a circle relates—22:7, symbolized as π (Pi).

Ruling Number 2

Only one total of numbers in a birth date will result in a Ruling Number 2 and that is the total of 20. (Totals of 29, 38, and 47 result in Ruling Number 11's.) Therefore, we find far fewer people with a Ruling 2 (and Ruling 22/4) than any other of the Ruling Numbers. The Ruling 2 is generally a sensitive, unassuming, supportive person.

Ruling Number 3

When we note its commanding position at the head of the Mind Plane, we realize why so much emphasis is placed on thinking and on reasoning by people whose Ruling Number is 3. These are people whose birth date numbers total 12, 21, 30, 39, or 48.

Ruling Number 4

In the modern world, where so much general emphasis is placed on material concerns, the basic expression of most people with a Ruling 4 can be easily gratified. But there is more to them than materialism, though their major emphasis certainly lies on the physical, the 4 being located in the center of the Physical Plane.

Ruling Number 5

In practice, we find that people with the Ruling Number 5 invariably strive to be free from constriction. This is a natural expression of their highly sensitive natures and their inherent need to express their feelings. It is not surprising when we realize that 5 is the center of the Soul Plane. Birth dates whose component numbers total 14, 23, 32, or 41 have a Ruling Number 5.

Ruling Number 6

This is a Ruling Number of extremes. These people have the potential for great creative power when living positively, yet they become incessant worriers when living negatively. The position of this number at the center of the Mind Plane gives Ruling 6 people tremendous potential to perceive and create brilliantly. Birth dates with component numbers totaling 15, 24, 33, or 42 have a Ruling Number 6.

Ruling Number 7

Under the influence of this Ruling Number, people gain maximum experience from life's lesson book, both through the personal sacrifice of learning and through teaching or sharing. Both facets of human growth are intimately related to physical expression. Birth dates with component numbers totaling 16, 25, 34, and 43 have a Ruling Number 7.

Ruling Number 8

These are people who regard independence as one of the most important aspects of life. They can be very complex people, who invariably possess great wisdom and strength of character.

Their power derives from the position of the 8 as the number of wisdom on the Soul Plane. Ruling Number 8 birth dates are those that total 17, 26, 35, or 44.

Ruling Number 9

The humanitarian qualities of ambition, responsibility, and idealism are the three-fold aspects of Ruling 9 people, whose prime motivation is to put people before things. They are individuals whose birth date numbers total 18, 27, 36, or 45.

Ruling Number 10

There is no greater range of expression than that found in the potential of the Ruling 10. They vary from the most likable, personality-plus people when living positively, to lost, floundering, insecure beings when negativity takes over. They are the most adaptable people. Birth dates with totals of 19, 28, 37, or 46 are Ruling 10's.

Ruling Number 11

An especially high level of spirituality surrounds this Ruling Number, offering those born to it a unique potential for developing the awareness of the High Self. Though we do not find a large amount of Ruling 11's, they proliferate in domains where personal and spiritual growth predominates.

In practice, only two birth date totals commonly qualify for Ruling number 11—29 and 38—though an occasional birth date total of 47 will be found.

Ruling Number 22/4

This is the master number. People born as 22/4's have almost limitless potential and often make their mark in life by achieving seemingly impossible goals. But there are two distinctly different Ruling 22/4's—the aware and the unaware. While the former benefit from the successful mastery of any aspect of life they choose, the latter drift into a lazy indifference, becoming almost useless misfits. Only one total of birth date numbers gives a Ruling Number 22/4 and that is 22, occurring with only one to two percent of the population.

DAY 10

Ruling Numbers: Life's Purpose and Best Expression

Today we are going to explore each Ruling Number's life purpose and best form of expression.

Ruling 2

Life's Purpose

These people have a special ability to work with and under the guidance of dynamic leadership. They are generally not leaders themselves, yet they have a unique ability to seek and associate with the type of organization or person who will appreciate their diligent capabilities. Their special role is to complement by providing loyal, intuitive support.

Best Expression

Though extremely capable and confident when allowed to work at their own pace, Ruling 2's can feel insecure if burdened with stress and urgency. They are exceptionally honorable and dislike their integrity being doubted. Their best expression is generally through the sensitive use of their hands, such as in art or in writing, but always guided by their intuition.

Ruling 3

Life's Purpose

As these people emphasize the thinking aspects of life, their primary purpose relates to their mental capabilities. For them, the understanding of life and the development of their personality are related to their thought processes. Their service to the community and their favored mode of expression is primarily expressed through thinking, planning, analyzing, memorizing, and so on.

Best Expression

The speed with which Ruling 3 people engage in mental work often leaves others behind. Their acute mental alertness is sometimes expressed in a keen sense of humor, a natural wit that makes them bright and intelligent company. It should be remembered that they invariably express themselves more fluently through the thinking channels than either emotionally or physically.

Ruling 4

Life's Purpose

While we continue to live on earth in a physical body, it is natural that so much of our experience is related to the material aspects of life. Ruling 4 people emphasize physical experience and expression. As they mature, their natural tendency is to become more practical, thereby giving themselves greater scope to develop love, awareness, and wisdom.

Best Expression

Ruling 4 people usually have extensive experience of physical or organizational work. It can range from the pleasure of making money as an end in itself, to the challenges of establishing gigantic business deals, through to the practical aspects of art and cultural affairs or an involvement in sporting events. Ruling 4's are generally more orthodox than adventurous. In general, they are the doers of the world.

Ruling 5

Life's Purpose

The mastery of sensitive expression through writing, painting, sculpture, and so on is one of the refinements of human endeavor.

However, it can only be achieved when adequate freedom prevails. It is just this type of expression that Ruling 5 people seek to develop as a means of acquiring the command of their emotions.

Best Expression

Most of these people find it difficult to work strictly regulated hours. They should seek work that allows them to be free of direction, as a traveling salesperson, freelance writer, or artist. Many feel the strong desire for adventure and love to travel or change jobs frequently. Many Ruling 5's also succeed as professional entertainers, but in whatever they do, their love of people is a primary motivation.

Ruling 6

Life's Purpose

Here we find people who excel in a wide range of creative endeavors, from the home to the global stage. All people with the Ruling 6 have a natural capacity for responsibility, but often they identify so strongly with it that anxiety and worry entrap them in a web of stress. They must learn to master situations rather than let the situations control them.

Best Expression

These people excel in positions where their trust, creativity, and sense of caring responsibility are called for. Some express these talents publicly, excelling with acting and/or singing on the stage or screen. Others utilize their loving nature in the home and with their family. At the core of their expression is always that deep love of humanity and a loving nature.

Ruling 7

Life's Purpose

The unique aspect of this Ruling Number is its almost limitless capacity for learning through personal involvement. Enlightenment acquired in such a manner invariably qualifies Ruling 7 people to capably share their experiences, making them excellent teachers. And the practical realization of their experiences equips them with a profound and abiding philosophy of life.

Best Expression

One of the most important requirements for Ruling 7 people is that they are allowed to learn *their* way, as they accept only minimum direction from others. This usually demands sacrifices in health, love, and/or money, and qualifies them as teachers and helpers of humankind. However, while they are not averse to implementing discipline in others, they find someone else's discipline difficult to live with.

Ruling 8

Life's Purpose

One of the most important aspects of love is our ability to express it. One of the most vital components of successful relationships is a fluent expression of appreciation. It is these two avenues of expression that Ruling 8 people find difficult. Growth in these directions will develop with the realization that improved relationships strengthen the confidence others have in them. In turn, this creates greater personal security and improved happiness in their lives, together with growth in wisdom.

Best Expression

Seemingly inconsistent for Ruling 8's is their enormous capacity for compassion and sympathetic tenderness for those in trouble. However, they grow impatient with anyone who becomes dependent upon them. They have the ability to be enormously successful in business, particularly if they do not let their emotions interfere with their commercial decision-making. They are feeling people who often hide their sensitivities until they become mature enough to express them.

Ruling 9

Life's Purpose

This is a powerful mind number implying a constant responsibility. They are far more suited to art than to science, to humanitarian rather than to commercial pursuits. Many of our cultural leaders and serious actors are found with this Ruling Number, all of whom are idealists at heart, though their concepts are not always the most workable. It is an important aspect of their purpose in life to learn to translate the idealistic into the practical.

Best Expression

To serve humanity and improve human life are at the very heart of a Ruling 9's expression. The method by which they can best achieve this will be found from the analysis of their Birth Chart (see Days 2–8) and Pyramids (see Days 16–17). These people are ambitious, but are more concerned with the overall plan than its details. They are thus more suited to non-commercial undertakings. They are very artistic, preferring serious to popular forms of artistic expression.

Ruling 10

Life's Purpose

Adaptability and adjustment are the keynotes of the Ruling 10's life. Their innate flexibility can be of enormous assistance when it comes to helping others adjust to life's changes and we find Ruling 10 people in a wide diversity of vocations and situations. They have a natural fearlessness that often leads them into pioneering ventures others would never consider undertaking.

Best Expression

If we want someone to assist us in enjoying the pleasures of life, we need look no further than a Ruling 10. Some Ruling 10 people are constantly forthright, non-reactive, and assertive—their optimism knows no bounds, leading them to achieve remarkable progress. This is the natural expression of the Ruling 10, being the powerful combination of the ego (the 1), expressing its infinite spiritual depth through the 0.

Ruling 11

Life's Purpose

These people are among the few who are best equipped to guide humanity into the emerging age of awareness. Unfortunately, many are enticed by life's physical attractions and are thus diverted from their higher purpose. But the tide is changing as the real values gain credence.

Best Expression

Ruling 11 people naturally gravitate toward an environment of beauty because it liberates them to express their innate spirituality. Material life, for them, can be uninteresting, but they have to learn to balance the material with their ideals to realize that the noblest spiritual virtues are of little value unless they can be used to improve the quality of life.

Ruling 22/4

Life's Purpose

There will always be people of outstanding leadership. In this New Age, the role of these people becomes crucial, for their personal enlightenment is a beacon whose light will illumine the Path and guide countless others. For centuries, 22/4's consistently chose to work behind the scenes, but more and more 22/4's are coming to the fore. They ask only for respect and cooperation to facilitate their work.

Best Expression

To achieve any semblance of their potential, Ruling 22/4's need a first-rate education. Many study a great deal, continually seeking to better themselves and to satisfy their craving for knowledge. The rate at which they learn is little short of amazing, as though they have accomplished most things in past lives and are merely reacquainting themselves with them. Little wonder they rise to leadership so often and are constantly called on for advice and guidance.

DAY 11

Ruling Numbers: Distinctive Traits and Negative Tendencies

Today we examine the distinctive traits and the negative tendencies of each Ruling Number.

Ruling 2

Distinctive Traits

Ruling 2's are intuitive, sensitive, reliable, diligent, and compassionate people. They are the peacemakers, sometimes to the extent of reforming. They are less motivated by ego than most people, being able to merge their ego with that of others when desirable or necessary.

Negative Tendencies to Be Surmounted

Some Ruling 2's fail to realize that their inherent development must result from personal involvement. Materialism or egocentricity will impel them to become discontented, irritable, and frustrated. They also rely too much on rationalization at the expense of intuition, which can lead to errors in judgment.

Ruling 3

Distinctive Traits

Their active brain, sense of humor, and mental alertness contribute to a successful working and social life for Ruling 3's. They are often the life of the party or the brightest person in the office, but this success does not always prevail at home, where they often become overly critical. Ruling 3's enjoy helping people, so long as they have the rapport on a mental level and the other people are prepared to cooperate.

Negative Tendencies to Be Surmounted

When not living constructively, these people often assume an air of superiority. Being so mentally alert, negative Ruling 3's readily show a lack of patience and an intolerance of others less blessed, becoming quite critical of their "limitations." This fault-finding can ultimately cause broken marriages.

Ruling 4

Distinctive Traits

These are people with a natural flair for the practical—they generally prefer to do a thing rather than discuss it. They are among the most systematic, reliable, and trustworthy people. This is especially evident in detailed work, where their accuracy and practical ability are second to none. On practical matters Ruling 4's can manifest extraordinary patience, but they are more impatient with intellectual or spiritual matters.

Negative Tendencies to Be Surmounted

It is quite common for Ruling 4's to become totally absorbed in their work and to neglect to bring balance to their lives. If they do not have a strong emotional equilibrium, they can easily lose heart due to frustrated ambition, leading to stress-induced illnesses. Should they neglect the need for a balanced life, an overly materialistic outlook could develop.

Ruling 5

Distinctive Traits

Ruling 5's are intuitive people with deep feelings and a strong artistic flair, who gain pleasure from expressing themselves. With such freedom, they are lively and dynamic; but if confined, they become sullen and moody, even apathetic. Yet they are usually good-natured people with a strong determination to enjoy life and to help others do so as well.

Negative Tendencies to Be Surmounted

Such a strong love of freedom can sometimes drive Ruling 5 people to take employment in illegal activities. Many young Ruling 5's rebel at having to answer to a boss and prefer to be unemployed. When inattentive to detail, Ruling 5's make poor business people, a problem exacerbated by their nervousness when confined to the workaday world.

Ruling 6

Distinctive Traits

Their exceptional creativity finds every opportunity to express itself at work, at play, and in the home. To Ruling 6 people, their home is the most important place. Great humanitarians, these people resent injustices of any kind. They are exceptionally loving, unselfish, and tolerant people who must guard against being imposed upon.

Negative Tendencies to Be Surmounted

When opportunities for expressing creativity are limited to the home, these people can suffer anxieties and possessiveness. This can lead to apprehensiveness and fear, such that their personal growth is severely constricted. When worry and negativity prevail in the lives of Ruling 6's, they adopt a whining voice and take on the air of fault-finder.

Ruling 7

Distinctive Traits

These people are among the most active. Though not always conscious of it, their driving force is the profound need for personal experience, and these experiences become most memorable when they comprise some form of sacrifice. These people possess a powerful, natural fortitude that often provides them with an inherent self-confidence that helps them handle their experiences more stoically than outsiders often realize. Their philosophy is that everything occurs for a purpose.

Negative Tendencies to Be Surmounted

Their compulsion for personal experience can cause Ruling 7's to become extremely rebellious. In refusing to accept advice, they adopt the attitude that they like to teach but they do not like to be taught. Until they mature and act with greater wisdom, their domestic and business lives will often be far from happy.

Ruling 8

Distinctive Traits

A strong air of independence and dependability, together with a self-confident manner, are distinctive of Ruling 8 people. These qualities work in harmony to equip them for positions of seniority and responsibility. But their fierce independence can often transmute to an attitude of coolness in the home. This is related to their difficulty in self-expression, an inhibition that usually diminishes with maturity. Their inherent love for helpless creatures—animals, infants, the elderly, and the sick—constantly seeks expression and instantly converts aloofness into loving kindness.

Negative Tendencies to Be Surmounted

Their fierce independence is so zealously guarded that these people develop a deep resentment toward any perceived form of interference with their plans. Ruling 8's need a great deal of guidance, especially in handling children—they are either overindulgent or exceptionally strict. They often find difficulty in love relationships, tending to hold their feelings in check. As they mature, they realize how much happier they can be when they express their feelings.

Ruling 9

Distinctive Traits

Ambition, responsibility, and idealism are their growth qualities, but through it all, the emphasis is on personal responsibility. Honesty is so natural to Ruling 9's that they assume everyone to be so inclined. This often leads to disappointments in people. They find it easier to give money to the needy, rather than save it for themselves, and this often frustrates their partners. Though their ideas are not always the most practical, Ruling 9's strive to implement them, such is their ambition and idealism.

Negative Tendencies to Be Surmounted

If Ruling 9's fail to adopt the ideals they seek to impress on others, they need to guard against being hypocritical. Their ambitions can dominate and destroy the integrity of their ideals, thereby developing an unattractive egocentricity. This will often produce an abrupt manner and a critical attitude, which the people in their lives will find difficult to tolerate and which can lead to their undoing when they are materially motivated.

Ruling 10

Distinctive Traits

Essentially a physical Ruling Number, the 10 endows a power of adaptability that produces a highly popular personality. Their generally happy disposition is quite contagious, yet they find it difficult to understand why others are not as happy. The aware minority becomes successful for they have a fortitude that enables them to rise above the most difficult conditions. In general, Ruling 10 people have an air of self-assurance, reflected in their personal confidence and their elegant appearance. They are generally artistic, with a sensitive touch that makes them competent instrumentalists.

Negative Tendencies to Be Surmounted

Their self-confidence can sometimes lead these people to dominate others, invariably creating disharmony. This tendency is best avoided through better control of the ego, recognizing the depth of spiritual substance, and avoiding superficiality. They must avoid being lazy and expecting life to be one big ball; and they must recognize the need to develop self-discipline to overcome melancholy and emotional insecurity.

Ruling 11

Distinctive Traits

There are extreme differences between the lifestyles of the Ruling 11's who live positively and utilize their spiritual powers and their negative counterparts whose lives appear difficult and colorless. An uncompromisingly high level of morality and ethics, a profoundly reliable intuitiveness, and an inspired driving force are clearly in evidence when these people are involved in spiritually-oriented pursuits. They are deeply feeling people, extremely dependable, honest, and just, with a deep love for family and friends and a sincere compassion for all life.

Negative Tendencies to Be Surmounted

When Ruling 11's stray from their life's Path, they become lost and apathetic. They must employ great awareness and care to be firm in their resolve to keep to their Path, for it will not be difficult so long as they listen to their profound intuition.

Ruling 22/4

Distinctive Traits

One of the most noticeable traits of the Ruling 22/4 is their apparent lack of emotion. Actually, they are very sensitive, highly intuitive people who combine the unique abilities of powerful spiritual awareness (the double 11) with the eminently practical 4. They rarely fail to accept a challenge, especially if it involves human welfare. They are found in some of the most difficult and seemingly dangerous environments. Their capacity for responsibility is almost limitless; consequently, some people habitually depend on them, often thoughtlessly.

Negative Tendencies to Be Surmounted

Most Ruling 22/4's readily recognize many of their strengths and capably employ them. The few who do not, or who are drawn into a materialistic environment, take on all the negative aspects of the Ruling 4, but worse. In so doing, they become little better than misfits, with an obsession for money. Rehabilitation demands great patience, understanding, and loving tenderness. As all Ruling 22/4's are fond of art, rhythm, dancing, and most forms of music, the wise use of these forms of expression will greatly help to bring a more positive attitude.

DAY 12

Ruling Numbers: Recommended Development

Our topic for today is the recommended development for each of the Ruling Numbers.

Ruling 2

Ruling 2's should employ their intuitive ability to develop self-confidence and to choose friends and associates who accept and appreciate their distinctive traits. It will be of considerable benefit to them to develop their mental faculties, especially their powers of deduction and memory. Such development will firmly anchor their self-esteem and provide greater personal happiness.

Ruling 3

Ruling 3 people must learn to develop sensitivity to the feelings of others. When they recognize that life's experiences provide constant learning and that they need to live with others in harmony, their success rate is greatly improved.

They must not blame others, but use their power of resilience to bounce back with vigor, looking upon "unfavorable" experiences as helpful opportunities for growth. They should broaden their means of expression by cultivating their intuitiveness and by being more practical in day-to-day affairs, especially around the home.

Ruling 4

Three important avenues of development for Ruling 4's are relaxation, mental application, and expanded intuitiveness. Relaxation is a vital means of detachment from material concerns and can also provide an excellent basis for mental and spiritual growth through meditation. Mental application in the forms of memory training and understanding principles, such as those taught in philosophy, engineering, and so on, will expand intuitive awareness, the doorway to spiritual consciousness. Ruling 4's should strive to balance their practicality with their mental and spiritual faculties.

Ruling 5

Ruling 5's need to develop attention to detail to gain a wider perspective on life, afforded by greater practicality. They will find it beneficial to travel and to develop their powers of observation. As they mature, their recognition of the importance of discipline will strengthen their personal security, especially in relationships. Ruling 5 people are love motivated, irrespective of how they represent themselves to the world, so they naturally respond to genuine appreciation and give it in return.

Ruling 6

Ruling 6 people must realize that a positive mental outlook is of utmost importance for developing creativity. Most Ruling 6's have a desire for peace at any price, but this can be a weakness, becoming self-destructive and leading to unhappiness. Developing a wise firmness will assist in guarding them against being imposed upon by thoughtless people. Distinguishing between the important and unimportant aspects of life, embracing an acute sense of temperance, and expressing their compassion wisely will all contribute to the more effective channeling of their powerful creative faculties.

Ruling 7

Ruling 7's are often not the best judges of character nor do they have sound business understanding, so they should be careful in matters of business and investment. But with wise self-discipline, these failings can be overcome—if only they would embrace as much discipline in their lives as they seek to impart to others. Generally, Ruling 7 people are slow learners, due to their need to experience so much for themselves. Parents should take special note of this characteristic and allow for their Ruling 7 children to learn at their own pace.

Ruling 8

Every effort should be made to overcome the undemonstrativeness Ruling 8's so often exhibit. As they learn to express their feelings more fluently, their happiness and personal security improve. With this growth will develop the overall wisdom that, hitherto, they have tended only to express in impersonal situations, such as in business or in giving advice to others. Their wisdom and maturity will be enhanced through travel, of which they are very fond.

Ruling 9

The strong idealism of the Ruling 9 does not make for a successful judge of character. Yet once this limitation is realized, it can be remedied by the study and employment of a reliable guide, such as numerology. This will assist them in investigating a person before drawing conclusions from their personal analysis. In turn, this study will help Ruling 9's develop their intuition and wisdom. Patience and persistence are two other important traits these people need to develop. Ruling 9's are seen as overly serious—they need to laugh more and enjoy humor as a vital balance.

Ruling 10

Ruling 10 people have the tendency to become lost in conformity and to accept mediocrity as the norm. They need to recognize their potential for the exceptional, their versatility, and their adaptability. Throughout their lives, they would be wise to practice meditation to center themselves. They should also employ temperance in their lives, and develop awareness of the world around them, harmony in their attitudes, compassion, and reverence for life.

Ruling 11

Spiritual faculties do not easily mix with commerce for the Ruling 11. Consequently, their best avenues for expression lie in professions that facilitate growth in spiritual awareness and give substance to their sensitivities. At the same time, adequate monetary rewards are essential, so a compromise is often in order. They have to learn not only the most practical means of expressing their spirituality, but also to be guided by intuition rather than motivated by egotistical desires. They are often tempted to reject assistance when in need, but must learn to be more receptive.

Ruling 22/4

For all Ruling 22/4 people, it is vital to ensure that life provides a balance of work and pleasure. Their considerable aptitude for work often causes them to become obsessed with achieving, to the detriment of quality family, hobby, and relaxation time. Their development along artistic lines through hobbies—such as singing, dancing, painting, writing, and so on—will enhance the expression of their feelings and relax them emotionally. They must realize they are never too old to learn, for learning is a lifelong pursuit.

DAY 13

Ruling Numbers: Suitable Vocations, Summary and Famous Examples

Today we consider the most suitable vocations for each Ruling Number, summarize their most significant qualities, and also learn of some famous examples.

Ruling 2

Most Suitable Vocations

These people are best suited to work as personal assistants to administrators, especially in charitable or educational activities. They are also artistic, expressing themselves through painting, music, song, or dance, but they feel more comfortable as part of a group, rather than as a soloist. They are sometimes found as diplomats, social workers, secretaries, and process workers.

Summary

Ruling 2's are sensitive, intuitive, supportive, reliable, peacemaking, compassionate, and artistic.

Famous Ruling 2's

- Prince Philip, born June 10, 1921

- Ronald Reagan, born February 6, 1911

- Julie Andrews, born October 1, 1935

Ruling 3

Most Suitable Vocations

Ruling 3 people are best suited to work in vocations that involve mental activity. This includes the academic fields, particularly the sciences, accountancy, business management, computer programming, systems analysis, and so on. They can be excellent research scientists and will also excel in some of the arts, such as writing and acting, or as critics of the arts.

Summary

These people enjoy entertaining others. Their minds are constantly alert and assessing, planning, and thinking. They possess intelligence and a sense of humor, yet can often experience marriage problems.

Famous Ruling 3's

- Channing Tatum, born April 26, 1980

- Kylie Minogue, born May 28, 1968

- Charles Dickens, born February 7, 1812

Ruling 4

Most Suitable Vocations

These people are best suited to work as skilled trades people, technicians, crafts people and machinists, as well as managers, professional sports people, economists, physicians, chiropractors, and horticulturists. In financial matters, they need to develop good judgment to ensure they are not motivated by personal avarice. Many teachers of manual arts, sports, and fitness, as well as authors of technical books and magazines, are found among Ruling 4's.

Summary

Ruling 4's are practical and conventional in outlook, often materialistic. They are interested in sports and very capable with their hands. They are "doing" people.

Famous Ruling 4's

- Arnold Schwarzenegger, born July 30, 1947

- Oprah Winfrey, born January 29, 1954

- Bill Gates, born October 28, 1955

Ruling 5

Most Suitable Vocations

Freedom, acting, and art summarize the essential Ruling 5 expression. This qualifies them best for working as acting professionals (whether on the stage or behind the scenes), as sales people, as politicians, in the travel or hospitality industries, or as writers, artists, entrepreneurs, designers, inventors, social workers, or reformers.

Summary

Their nature is essentially loving and freedom-loving; artistic, adventurous, and moody; jovial when free to be expressive and sullen when feeling restricted. Essentially, they are "feeling" people.

Famous Ruling 5's

- Abraham Lincoln, born February 12, 1809

- Vincent van Gogh, born March 30, 1853

- Angelina Jolie, born June 4, 1975

Ruling 6

Most Suitable Vocations

Whatever they do they must have creative prospects that are directly or ultimately designated for the betterment of human welfare. They excel in humanitarian organizations, and as healers, artists, and designers. They have a remarkable ability for dramatic singing and acting.

Summary

Ruling 6 people are creative, caring, just, unselfish, tolerant, and home loving, but inclined toward deep worry and anxiety.

Famous Ruling 6's

- Agatha Christie, born September 15, 1890

- Meryl Streep, born June 22, 1949

- Eddie Murphy, born April 3, 1961

Ruling 7

Most Suitable Vocations

Trustworthy, and expecting trust from others, these people are well suited to positions among the judiciary and in legal practice. They are practical people, often choosing careers as surgeons, butchers, and carpenters. Ruling 7's are also found as teachers and as clergy, scientists, naturalists, and philosophers.

Summary

Ruling 7's need to learn through personal experience, but dislike external discipline. They are assertive, philosophical, and humanitarian. Their lives incur an unusually high level of sacrifice.

Famous Ruling 7's

- Marilyn Monroe, born June 1, 1926

- Julia Roberts, born October 28, 1967

- Leonardo DiCaprio, born November 11, 1974

Ruling 8

Most Suitable Vocations

Ruling 8's are often found at the head of large business undertakings, or as senior executives. They are attracted to banking, stock-broking, and so on. They will also be found as travel executives, aircraft and ship's captains, teachers and nurses, working with animals or as senior figures of humane organizations. Due to their ability to mask their natural feelings, many become successful at professional acting.

Summary

They are independent, highly dependable, self-confident, undemonstrative, commercially oriented and deeply concerned for the sick and the helpless.

Famous Ruling 8's

- Whoopi Goldberg, born November 13, 1955
- Nelson Mandela, born July 18, 1918
- Sandra Bullock, born July 26, 1964

Ruling 9

Most Suitable Vocations

Ruling 9's will be found happily working in religious disciplines, welfare organizations, educational institutions (as administrators rather than teachers), research facilities, crime solving, the healing professions, and as counselors. Many will be found in professional acting and artistic careers, but in the more serious aspects of them. They rarely excel as senior business executives.

Summary

Ruling 9's are eminently responsible, extremely honest, idealistic, ambitious, humanitarian, and very serious about life. They have difficulty saving money.

Famous Ruling 9's

- Mother Teresa, born August 26, 1910

- Elvis Presley, born January 8, 1935

- Morgan Freeman, born June 1, 1937

Ruling 10

Most Suitable Vocations

The fields of professional sports or entertainment, interior decorating and design, and work with fabrics or food are good vocations for Ruling 10's. Also, they make good salespeople, politicians, charity fundraisers, business executives, sales managers, town planners, architects, and real estate agents.

Summary

They are confident, debonair, bright, and happy people, with a sensitive touch and an amazing ability to sell.

Famous Ruling 10's

- Steve Jobs, born February 24, 1955
- Tom Hanks, born July 9, 1956
- Henry Ford, born July 30, 1863

Ruling 11

Most Suitable Vocations

Educators, social workers, religious leaders, and personal growth instructors are often found to be Ruling 11's. Others teach cultural subjects, and work in exploration and the field of professional performing. Their intuition can make them amazing designers or inventors.

Summary

The Ruling 11's are sensitive, feeling, and caring people. They love refinement, beauty, and everything with a depth of cultural substance, and are intensely honest and compassionate, often preferring to avoid business, for they are generally not competent money managers.

Famous Ruling 11's

- Wolfgang Amadeus Mozart, born January 27, 1756
- Jennifer Aniston, born February 11, 1969
- Barack Obama, born August 4, 1961

Ruling 22/4

Most Suitable Vocations

These people are suited to work as leaders in practically any business or cultural organization. They excel at whatever they attempt, be it in art, writing, politics, the diplomatic services, or as humanitarians, technicians (especially with computers), or teachers.

Summary

This is the master number, whose bearers have the most responsibility to humanity. They are self-confident, highly intuitive, and sensitive, with a tight rein on their emotions and an intense concern for human welfare. They have to take care not to become ruthless in pursuit of their goals.

Famous Ruling 22/4's

- Leonardo da Vinci, born April 15, 1452

- Frank Sinatra, born December 12, 1915

- Kim Kardashian, born October 21, 1980

DAY 14

Introducing the Day Numbers

Today we are going to examine how we present our outer selves to the world.

Just as it is important for us to develop the understanding of our eternal being, the inner self, so is it necessary for us to understand the manner by which we express ourselves to the world through the outer self. We do this through our Day Number and our name (see Day 18).

With most birth dates, the Day Number is different from the Ruling Number. Yet for some people it is the same number. In these instances, the apparent need to strengthen your Ruling Number clearly outweighs the need to divert from it.

To prepare it for proper analysis, each Day Number is treated in the same basic manner as the Ruling Number. Each double number of a day on which a person is born is resolved to a single number by simple addition, with the same exceptions as the Ruling Number. However, there is one additional exception for a Day Number, and it occurs when a person is born on the first day of the month. We do not have a Ruling Number 1, but we certainly have a Day Number 1. To avoid any misunderstandings, I have listed all the Day Numbers in the table opposite.

Because each number has the same basic properties, a Day Number will have similar aspects to its identical Ruling Number, except that the Ruling Number is naturally the stronger. It is important to realize that the Day Number is intended to represent our alternate other self. Thus, when people choose to align themselves more with its power than that of their Ruling Number, their lives will ultimately fall apart.

Day Born	Day Number	Day Born	Day Number
1st day of month	1	17th day of month	8
2nd day of month	2	18th day of month	9
3rd day of month	3	19th day of month	10
4th day of month	4	20th day of month	2
5th day of month	5	21st day of month	3
6th day of month	6	22nd day of month	22/4
7th day of month	7	23rd day of month	5
8th day of month	8	24th day of month	6
9th day of month	9	25th day of month	7
10th day of month	10	26th day of month	8
11th day of month	11	27th day of month	9
12th day of month	3	28th day of month	10
13th day of month	4	29th day of month	11
14th day of month	5	30th day of month	3
15th day of month	6	31st day of month	4
16th day of month	7		

DAY 15

A Guide to the Day Numbers

Today we explore the meanings of each of the Day Numbers.

Day Number 1

People born on the first day of the month always do their best when allowed to work on their own. They need freedom to develop and express their unique initiative. The direction in which to channel this expression is indicated by their Ruling Number. Because of their preference for individual effort, these people can appear aloof or detached.

Day Number 2

This brings with it added intuitiveness, which is valuable in decision-making. These people enjoy light entertainment, especially if humorous, preferring to be entertained than to do the entertaining. They are reliable, supportive people who are generally lighthearted, preferring the natural to the artificial.

Day Number 3

These people are fun-loving entertainers. They thoroughly enjoy all forms of humor, especially satirical humor. They are generally bright extroverts with a very active brain and a ready answer, but they do have an underlying tendency to be critical of more somber people without attempting to understand such different personalities.

Day Number 4

A practical and capable flair helps these people to express themselves well with their hands or feet. If their Ruling Number is an odd number, this Day Number will assist them in creating balance through a predominantly artistic or philosophical approach to life. Should their Ruling Number be an even number, they need to take care to avoid materialism, and learn that they will achieve the best results when they employ their ability to organize.

Day Number 5

These are caring, compassionate people who need the freedom to express their deep feelings. They are sensitive and able to achieve success and happiness, provided they do not develop a fear of being misunderstood. This could produce a shyness that inhibits their true self-expression. They need plenty of outdoor exercise and activity, and to select bright company with whom they can share laughter and joy.

Day Number 6

Though this is a number of creativity, for most people such expression seems to be restricted to the domestic sphere. This is especially so in the case of women. This number's positive expression is through love and beauty, qualities that inspire a person to brighten up the home or the workplace. When living negatively, these people overdramatize domestic problems and develop fears. Their panacea is readily found by replacing the worry habit with creativity.

Day Number 7

No number provides a more active understanding of life's lessons than the 7. Its special purpose is to induce personal involvement where the person learns the lessons of life in the most indelible way—through personal sacrifice. This will usually affect the pocket more than health or love, though the latter two will be involved if the lessons are not readily recognized. As these people mature in wisdom, they will share their life's experiences through teaching.

Day Number 8

As Day Number 8's grow in personal awareness, they recognize an emerging need for the independent expression of their feelings, emotions, and intuition. This independence is the basis upon which all other forms of personal expression depend. However, some people misconstrue financial independence as the basis. Unless financial success is based on a mature understanding of their personal life, such prosperity will be temporary.

Day Number 9

In its more limited role as a Day Number, the 9 expresses itself primarily as the symbol of responsibility, motivated by idealism. This tends to imply a rather serious role in our affairs, but it is not intended that we be constantly serious, as are so many people with this Day Number. If such is the case, they should seek happy company, learning to have fun and laugh more to maintain that vital emotional balance.

Day Number 10

These people are gregarious, energetic, generous, and easily pleased. But they need to guard against a tendency toward superficiality, for this inhibits the development of worthwhile friendships and restricts their personal understanding of the real purpose of life. They should be prepared to use their talents to develop their primary purpose in life, as revealed by their Ruling Number.

Day Number 11

The high level of spirituality with which this number is identified usually finds its best expression through intuition as a Day Number. Unfortunately, a tendency of so many Day Number 11 people is to become involved in emotional extremes, expressed in moodiness, anxiety, or abruptness. These emotions are enervating and unhealthy. They should be controlled as soon as they are recognized, for they can be easily transformed to become positive spiritual guidance.

Day Number 22/4

The potential power of this number is second to none, for it combines intuition with practicality, leading to the recognition that anything is possible. But this will only become a reality if the person has achieved a comprehensive integration of the

Mind, Soul, and Physical Planes. Otherwise, their motivation can become a base desire to attain power. Such is the temptation for people of this Day Number, and they need to remember that the Day Number is essentially an alternate power and is never intended to be the primary influence.

DAY 16

Setting Up Your Number Pyramid

Today we learn how to create our Number Pyramid.

To the ancient masters, pyramids had profound significance. Symbolically, they represented the humans' aspirations toward their Creator and to ultimate perfection. Materially, they were constructed to attract and focus enormous power, as well as to perpetuate the secrets of eternal life. The total construction was not meant to be merely an impressive funereal edifice. It was instead a gigantic power source within which the knowledge and wisdom of the buried leaders could be amplified and then spiritually transmitted throughout the nation, thereby perpetuating their omniscient influence over the affairs of the people.

The mode of construction of the pyramids also involved the ancient mysteries, many of which remain undiscovered even today. But what we do know is that the ancient symbolism, as represented by these noble structures, was adapted by Pythagoras, in consequence of his deep studies, to be representative of the other most noble structures, the human body in its maturing state.

Four Pyramids are constructed to represent human life through the years of maturity. These represent a period of 27 years, comprising three cycles, each of nine years. The age at which each person commences their ascent of the Pyramids is found by deducting their Ruling Number from the mystical number, 36. This number had a special significance in the design and construction of the ancient pyramids, representing as it does the square of 6, the number of creation. It also has a special significance for Biblical scholars, for it is the number of chapters of the fourth book of the Bible—the name of which is Numbers.

To illustrate the construction of the Pyramids for human birth dates, the following step-by-step method is offered. It is the simplest and most reliable means to learn the construction, so readers should be prepared to follow it precisely and to practice it on the birth dates of every person they can. For convenience, I have chosen the birth date of Queen Elizabeth II—April 21, 1926—as the example.

Step 1

Reduce the birth date to single digits for each of the three factors—month, day, year—ensuring that they are kept separate. Then place them in order as just described, the month placed first because it has the least strength of the three numbers. Thus, the month in our example is 4, the day is reduced to 3 (2 + 1 = 3) and the year is reduced to 9 (1 + 9 + 2 + 6 = 18; 1 + 8 =9). The three numbers are then set out as follows, forming the base numbers upon which the Pyramids are to be constructed:

4 3 9

Step 2

Build the first Pyramid based on the first two numbers as follows:

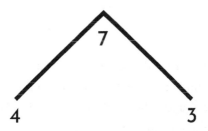

The Peak Number for this Pyramid is found by adding together the two numbers at the base of the Pyramid and, if necessary, resolving them to a single digit. But in this example it is already a single digit—7 is therefore placed inside the first peak unchanged. (If the base numbers were 7 and 8, the Peak Number would be 6, the total of 7 and 8 resolved to a single digit.)

Step 3

Build the second Pyramid on the second and third base numbers:

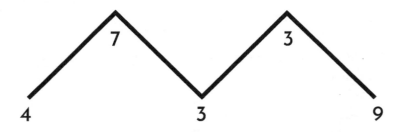

The Peak Number for this second Pyramid is found by adding 3 and 9, the numbers at the base. These total 12, which has to be resolved to a single digit by adding 1 and 2. Thus, the Peak Number for the second Pyramid is 3.

Step 4

Build the third Pyramid on the two existing Pyramids:

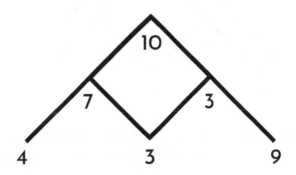

The Peak Number of the third Pyramid is the total of the first and second Peak Numbers. This is also resolved to a single digit, except if the total is 10 or 11, in which case it remains as these full numbers. Our example shows that Queen Elizabeth II's third Peak Number was 10.

Step 5

The final Pyramid is built around the other three because its base numbers are the first and third—4 and 9 in this example:

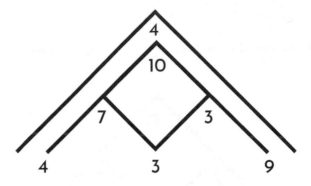

The Peak Number for this fourth Pyramid is the total of its two base numbers, 4 and 9, being 13. As with the other peaks, this is resolved to a single digit, resulting in a Peak Number of 4; but if the total were 10 or 11 they would not be reduced. It is important to note that these two double numbers are only used if they appear on the third or fourth peaks, for here their stronger spiritual influence has special importance as the third phase of life is approached.

Step 6

We now have four Pyramids, representing Queen Elizabeth II's second stage of life—maturity. The peak of each Pyramid indicates very important years in the period of the Queen's maturity. The age at which she reached the first peak is the chronological age at which her second stage of life (maturity) began. This is found by deducting her Ruling Number, 7, from 36. Thus, the age of 29 is placed adjacent to the first peak, together with the year at which this age is reached, viz. 1955.

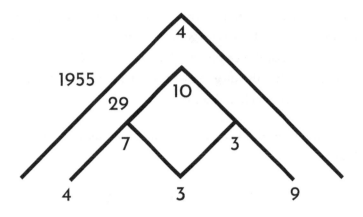

The ages attained at the remaining Pyramid peaks advance in nine-year intervals. Thus, the second peak is reached at age 38 in the year 1964; the third peak at age 47 in 1973; the fourth peak at age 56 in 1982. When these numbers are placed on the Pyramid diagram, it is completed as follows:

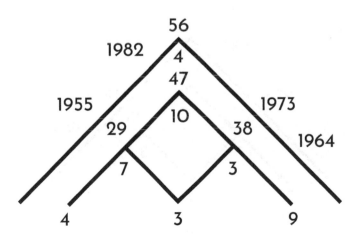

As an exercise to ensure you completely understand this important method, take a large piece of paper and write on it the birth date of Prince Philip—June 10, 1921. Now close the book and set up the diagram of his Pyramids; then check to see how much you have learned.

The complete Birth Chart and the Pyramids for Prince Philip is:

$$6 + 1 + 0 + 1 + 9 + 2 + 1 = 20/2$$

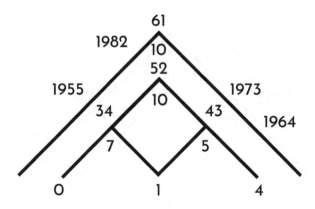

If your efforts did not result in an identical diagram, it is suggested that you recheck your methods step by step. It is important that these methods be thoroughly understood before further progress can be made.

We must also be certain of the year that each Pyramid starts and the ages at which people of each Ruling Number arrive at their peaks. The following chart illustrates this for those who do not wish to do their own calculation:

Ruling Number of person	Age at first peak	Age at second peak	Age at third peak	Age at fourth peak
2	34	43	52	61
3	33	42	51	60
4	32	41	50	59
5	31	40	49	58
6	30	39	48	57
7	29	38	47	56
8	28	37	46	55
9	27	36	45	54
10	26	35	44	53
11	25	34	43	52
22/4	32	41	50	59

DAY 17

Interpreting the Peak Numbers

Now that we are familiar with the setting-up of the Pyramids, today we will learn what they have to teach us. The most important set of numbers to be considered are the four Peak Numbers.

The Peak Numbers

Due to the contrasting conditions necessary for each of us to achieve a well-balanced maturity, we need additional help to that normally available from the Ruling Number. We get our supplementary support from the four Peak Numbers on our Pyramids. The object of the Peak Numbers is to provide a valuable source of additional thrust at specific periods during the maturing years.

Peak Number 1 will only be found on either the first or the second Pyramids (or occasionally on both). On the third or the fourth Pyramids, it becomes a 10. The 1 is an intensely practical number, indicating a period of individual effort and personal expression. For most it will mean separation from previous involvements in which disharmony was inhibiting personal development, such as in marriage or business. Some people will avoid such separations, but they will see a change in the relationship because they begin to exert more individuality and become more expressive. The direction of their activities is usually consistent with their Ruling Number; the manner in which they express themselves will depend on their Birth Chart.

Peak Number 2 introduces a period when stronger spiritual values emerge. Lifestyle and habits will subtly embrace either a more intuitive or a more emotional manner. Whether the spiritual emphasis manifests as an improved state of awareness or as a state of heightened emotions will depend on the level of maturity thus far achieved. Remember, there is a right time for everything, and one of the most important applications of numerology is to learn what our needs are and the right way, as well as the right time, to deal with them. To enforce material progress when under the influence of the Peak Number 2 would be to invite frustration, conflict, and emotional enervation.

Peak Number 3 is always a period when the emphasis should be directed toward intellectual pursuits. It is an important period of learning, reviewing, and analyzing. Many people find the urge for travel particularly accentuated under the guidance of this vibration. At this period in their lives, travel for such people assumes a very important role as a means of learning and expanding their insight into life. If they do not allow their mental faculties scope for positive expansion, they run the risk of becoming destructively critical, exacting, and unpopular.

Peak Number 4 brings with it increased material power. This might be expressed in a number of ways, depending upon the general level of maturity, Ruling Number, and Birth Chart characteristics. For those who need to acquire additional knowledge of the sense faculties to round off their maturity and who are prepared to involve themselves in physical work, vital development will reward their efforts. But those who become overly ambitious, mercenary, or covetous will find this period one of loss, rather than gain.

Peak Number 5 usually introduces significant changes to people's emotional state. These are created through the emergence of spiritual growth and understanding, which leads to greater personal freedom. It is a period through which psychic powers strengthen considerably, thereby facilitating an improved level of emotional control. As a consequence, a greater measure of personal liberty develops that prepares the way for increased spiritual awareness. Those who in earlier years were anxious about their financial security now have the means to dispel such worry with a more balanced view of their real needs.

Peak Number 6 brings with it a very strong power for creative development. It is a period when the highest spiritual and mental faculties can combine to reveal our vital role in the plan of creation. Such sublime awareness will rarely become apparent to any but the more mature, more highly evolved people. For the majority, those who identify with physical possessiveness, this becomes a period of intense home involvement or a hankering to settle down in their own home. Wisdom and patience should be exercised to avoid the need for the hurtful lessons that are attracted when emotions dominate people's affairs.

Peak Number 7 can bring many surprising changes into people's lives. It is the period when we are called upon to share all we have learned so far. By so doing, we experience tremendous progress ourselves, for there is no better system of learning than teaching. This period in life requires us to undergo much testing. If successful, we qualify for the higher teachings that await us; if not, we must spend more time in preparatory development. Most people are called upon to undertake some form of teaching during this period, often associated with fields of human evolvement such as yoga, natural therapies, spiritual awareness, and artistic development.

Peak Number 8 denotes independence as the prevailing force during this powerful period. Whether independence develops through artistic or commercial involvements will depend on the Ruling Number: if it is an even number, financial success if indicated; if an odd number, success through artistic (or for some people, academic) expression is more likely. Great care must be taken to use the power of this vibration constructively, and not let opposing individuals or limiting situations inhibit its transmission.

Peak Number 9 introduces a period of pronounced humanitarian activity. This vibration brings with it special opportunities to serve humankind. It is also a period when intense mental involvement is necessary for the greatest success to be achieved: analyzing and assessing the needs of others, planning major changes in vocation, and re-evaluating long-standing relationships and environmental surroundings. While some people under this vibration will need to remain at home and be of service, others will be moved to travel to undergo important lessons in development.

Peak Number 10 can only occur on the third or fourth Pyramid peaks, as maturity approaches its zenith. It brings a special strength, a unique power for relating to the needs of others during important periods of adjustment in their lives. This ability is the happy consequence of people's own life experiences and the training instilled by them. With the emphasis on mind power, as indicated by the 9 in every birth date last century, a considerable amount of mental adjustment is needed to remold outlooks and lifestyles as the New Age approaches. Older souls who have a Peak Number 10 during this period assume critically important roles in guiding and encouraging those in need. This is an exciting responsibility that confers upon the giver as many benefits as upon the receiver.

Peak Number 11 is the second of the two Peak Numbers that can occur on either the third or fourth peaks. As with the Peak Number 10, a high level of maturity is necessary to handle its power. Peak Number 11 indicates that a considerable amount of spiritual accountability is demanded. Yet the demand will never exceed the individual's capacity. It is a period of high intuitiveness, when the most inspired actions become possible. However, there are certain spiritual requirements necessary for the optimum potential of this period to be realized. These involve compassion, temperance, integrity, and the practice of meditation.

DAY 18

The Power of Names

Today our topic is the numerological power of names.

A name is important because its vibrations become fused with our own. The term "vibration" applies to not only the audible wave frequencies but, even more broadly, the symbolic vibrations of the name as indicated by its numerological pattern. These vibrations exert an influence on our very personality and individuality.

The force exerted by names on the molding of the personality will primarily depend upon the strength of the name and its relationship to the Ruling Number of the person. If they have a less-than-powerful birth date, the influence of their name will be far greater than if the reverse applied. This is particularly exemplified in the life of the sixteenth president of the United States, Abraham Lincoln. His birth date (February 12, 1809) was not powerful, but his name gave the strength he needed to overcome personality weaknesses and achieve a lasting place in history. By contrast, a powerful birth date, such as December 27, 1935, and the name John will find very little influence exercised upon the personality by the name.

Irrespective of age, all people respond to some degree to the vibrations of their names. This response is greatest during the impressionable years of infancy and adolescence. Indeed, it can be of great help to children if parents are numerologically guided in the selection of their children's names. Personalities will be more balanced if the name and birth date harmonize.

To assess the power of a name, we must start by obtaining its numerological values. This is achieved by translating the letters of the name to their equivalent numbers using the following table:

1	2	3	4	5	6	7	8	9
A	B	C	D	E	F	G	H	I
J	K	L	M	N	O	P	Q	R
S	T	U	V	W	X	Y	Z	

As A is the first letter of the alphabet, it is equivalent to the first number of the numerical scale, the number 1. Each successive letter after A relates to the equivalent number following 1. So, B is equivalent to 2, C to 3, D to 4, and so on, to the last letter of the alphabet.

When analyzing names, we are concerned only with the used names. It is of little more than academic interest to analyze a given name or a family name (surname) if it is not used by the person. Our interest lies in analyzing whatever name is used in daily life, for used names are living names, and only living names have a vibrational influence on the inner self. For instance, Alan might prefer to be called Al or Samantha might prefer Sam.

In other examples, people have been known to dislike their first name, preferring to be known by their middle name. Others might dislike both their first and middle names, preferring to be known only by the initials of both. This is popular in some of the southern states of the U.S., where, for instance, a person called Jacob Benjamin might be known simply as J. B.—we would then analyze JB as his first name.

The analysis of rejected names will often throw an interesting light on the personalities that rejected them, indicating the reason for the change. There might also be environmental reasons—the name associated with people, places, or social attitudes they dislike. These can also often be numerologically explained. It is always illuminating to compare the reason given by the people for the change with that revealed by numerological analysis.

Practice will reveal that a different degree of emphasis will exist between a person's used first name and their family name. As a rule, the first name is used more in personal affairs, so it has greater impact on the personality. Family names are used more frequently in business or professional circles, hence their greater influence in these fields. These points should be recognized when the analysis is being made.

In translating the first name, middle name, or a nickname to its numerological equivalent, we adopt a simple method of separating the number of consonants from vowels. This enables us to easily obtain the totals of vowel numbers and consonant numbers separately. From the separate totals, we can gain an understanding of the name's influence on the personality in terms of its Soul Urge (vowels) and its Outer Expression (consonants). Then by adding these two totals we obtain the Ruling Number equivalent of the name, the Complete Name Number. Please note that a double first name (for example, Sally-Anne) or a hyphenated surname are to be analyzed as one name.

Examples of the following three names (shown opposite) will indicate how the upper line of numbers represents the vowels of each name. When totaled, these provide the Soul Urge Number.

1			1		1		3		
A	B	R	A	H	A	M		26/8	
	2	9		8		4	23/5		

5		9		1		5		20/2	
E	L	I	Z	A	B	E	T	H	43/7
	3		8		2		2	8	23/5

	6			6		
J	O	H	N		20/2	
1		8	5	14/5		

The lower line of numbers represents the consonants and, by their totals, the Outer Expression Number is obtained as shown above.

DAY 19

Soul Urge Numbers

Today we delve deeper into Soul Urge Numbers.

In the same way the individual numbers of the birth date are added to obtain the Ruling Number, individual numbers of each vowel in a name are added to obtain the Soul Urge Number, as indicated by the vowel numbers. The Soul Urge Number of the name Abraham is 3; Elizabeth is 2; John is 6, as we saw in the examples we looked at yesterday. This method is followed for each of the used names of a person.

Vowels are the soul of a word—its life, so to speak. Every trained singer, actor, and speaker recognizes this. It is therefore apparent that the vowel numbers of a person's name bear a close relationship to that person's inner feelings, the nature of which is discernible from the total number of the vowel numbers, known appropriately as the Soul Urge Number.

From the Soul Urge Number of a given name we learn some of the more subtle aspects of the individual's spiritual sensitivity, fortitude, and drive. These can be expressed in a number of ways: through feelings, emotions, desires, fancies, and so on. The forms of expression will vary with each Soul Urge Number.

Soul Urge 1

This appears only in names containing the single vowel "A": Ann, Jack, Jan, and Chad. The need for individual freedom of expression is indicated here. The means by which this can be achieved will be demonstrated best by the person's Ruling Number. In general, this Soul Urge Number implies a strong desire for freedom; that is, sufficient time to themselves, either to relax or undertake some kind of personal artistic expression.

Soul Urge 2

Representative names are Anna, Elizabeth, Adam, and Oliver—vowel numbers totaling either 2 or 20. Here is an urge to do things in a balanced way so that harmony prevails in every expression. These are generally quite intuitive people, with a strong preference for the natural over the artificial. In their dealings with other people, they are very fair and, by the same token, expect the same in return.

Soul Urge 3

Representative names are Amanda, Joanne, and Samantha—vowel numbers totaling 3, 12, or 21. With its emphasis always anchored on the mental, 3 as a Soul Urge Number combines feeling with thinking and assessing. The result is generally a capable appraisal of people and situations. This can be highly beneficial in business and professional activities.

Soul Urge 4

Representative names are Stuart, Una, Angus, and Paul—vowel numbers totaling either 4 or 13. When the practical 4 is expressed at the soul level, it indicates that the individual has very orderly, conservative opinions on a wide range of spiritual and emotional subjects embracing religion, love, marriage, and life in general. They are usually quite orthodox in outlook and not given to emotional outbursts.

Soul Urge 5

Representative names are Mike, Shirley, Keith, and Drew—vowel numbers totaling either 5 or 14. With its natural strength derived from its location on the Soul Plane, the occurrence of 5 as a Soul Urge Number indicates great depth of feeling and the need for freedom and acceptance. Whatever the aspect of life involved, these people will invariably feel strongly about it and will have their say on the matter.

Soul Urge 6

Representative names are Charles, Allen, Megan, and Jane—vowel numbers totaling either 6 or 15. Love and creativity are the operative words here. For these people, every opportunity to express themselves creatively should be taken, whether at work, with a hobby, or in the home. Their strength will decline into despair and torment if they lapse into overanxiety.

Soul Urge 7

Representative names are Joan, Angela, Hamilton, and Marianne—vowel numbers totaling either 7 or 16. The urge to teach and to help others is the predominant driving force here. However, these people do not take too kindly to others teaching them, preferring to learn by their own experiences. They often pay dearly for this privilege until they come to the realization that human beings are intended to help each other in a two-way relationship.

Soul Urge 8

Representative names are Joanna, Bruce, and Jonathan—vowel numbers totaling either 8 or 17. More than wishing to act independently, these people tend to mentally disassociate from unconventionally accepted habits, if such habits do not seem reasonable to them. They evidence a strong preference for individual thought and freedom but must guard against becoming aloof. One important lesson life teaches us is the need to participate in society without necessarily being bound by it.

Soul Urge 9

Representative names are Samuel, Claude, and Jim—vowel numbers totaling 9 or 18. When living positively, these people always seek to improve the quality of life, guided by a keen sense of humanitarian responsibility. If living negatively, they tend to become overly ambitious, with an unbalanced idealism that nags them to engage in many egocentric (and often unsuccessful) acts. The power of this number should be respected and utilized altruistically, otherwise it can become a savage taskmaster.

Soul Urge 10

Representative names are Lisa, Craig, David, and Douglas—vowel numbers totaling either 10 or 19. Metaphysical flexibility is the power conferred by this number. It offers the ability to bring into play a wide range of soul-oriented powers. Putting to use such metaphysical endowments as intuition, clairvoyance, clairaudience, thought transference, and astral projection will negate many of the limitations society places on these people. To employ any of these faculties in daily life constructively emancipates these people and brings awareness of the divinity within human beings, the essence of life.

Soul Urge 11

Representative names are Robert, Errol, and Cleo—vowel numbers totaling 11 only. The special spiritual qualities of the 11 are apparent here. As a Soul Urge Number, it offers a valuable intuitive strength that is especially beneficial if the individual does not have intuitive strength indicated on the Birth Chart or as part of their Ruling Number. It also serves to increase compassion, an ability to attune to other people's feelings.

How to Analyze the "Y"

Numerologically, the Y is usually considered a consonant, with the value of 7. It will ordinarily appear as an Outer Expression Number (see Day 20), exemplified in such names as Kelly, Sally, and Shirley. However, the exception arises in a name in which the Y is pronounced as "I" or "E" with no actual vowel appearing in the name. Then, and only then, do we analyze the Y as a vowel, thereby giving the name a Soul Urge Number of 7, as in Lyn and Ty, or the surnames Byrd, Hynd, and Lynch.

DAY 20

Outer Expression and Complete Name Numbers

Today our subjects are the Outer Expression Numbers and Complete Name Numbers.

Obtaining the value of the Outer Expression Number follows the same pattern we established yesterday for Soul Urge Numbers. By adding together the numerical values of the consonants below the name, their total is obtained then easily converted to its single digit equivalent, which we now recognize as the Outer Expression Number.

Like the Soul Urge Numbers, the Outer Expression Numbers range from 1 to 11, with the additional number of 22/4. Names in the English language generally possess insufficient vowels to total 22; however, it is not uncommon to find names with consonants that give this total. Characteristics associated with each of the Outer Expression Numbers are:

Outer Expression 1

This can only occur with names that have the single consonant J or S. Few given names comply with this limitation but among those that do, Sue and Joe are the most commonly used. These are people, such as the solo sports person or solo worker, who need the freedom to set their own pace in order achieve great satisfaction and develop their self-confidence in physical activities.

Outer Expression 2

Examples of names are Samantha, Jose, and Nicholas—names with consonant number totals of either 2 or 20. Indicated here is the preference to work as part of a group in happy surroundings. They are bright people with a desire for fun and lighthearted pleasures. This does not imply that they are shallow, but rather that they have a great capacity to enjoy organized activity.

Outer Expression 3

Examples of names are Sacha, Keith, Jody, and Beth—names with consonant number totals of 3, 12, 21, or 30. The Outer

Expression Number of 3 reveals the person as an entertainer. They derive great pleasure and give much to others, for they usually have a quick wit and a bright outlook.

Outer Expression 4

Examples of names are Eloise, Ada, Rod, and Angus—names with consonant number totals of 4, 13, or 31. This is an intensely practical number that belongs to active people who seek involvement with their hands, feet, or bodies. They specifically enjoy sports and building or repairing things.

Outer Expression 5

Examples of names are Andrew, Stuart, and Rachel—names with consonant number totals of 5, 14, 23, or 32. Freedom from physical confinement is the oft-expressed need of these people. To avoid frustration, they should seek a job that does not confine them, and the company of responsive, uninhibited people.

Outer Expression 6

Examples of names are James, Jane, Douglas, and Angela—names with consonant number totals of 6, 15, 24, or 33. The tendency to focus much of their energy and attention on the home is the ever-present characteristic here. Caution must be used to avoid overindulgence by maintaining a practical balance between pampering and attending to the more realistic needs of the domestic circle.

Outer Expression 7

Examples of names are Oliver, Philip, and Megan—names with consonant number totals of 7, 16, 25, or 34. These people have the compulsion to do things themselves, being strongly motivated toward personal involvement and learning on their own terms, in their own way.

Outer Expression 8

Examples of names are Adam, Samuel, and Bill—names with consonant number totals of 8, 17, 26, or 35. These are people who elect to act individually, to the extent that they dare to be different if the need demands it. In this manner, they assert their strong personalities, for they are aware that humans can never achieve a high level of self-development when identified with the herd mind.

Outer Expression 9

Examples of names are Sarah, Pat, and Don—names with consonant totals of 9, 18, 27, or 36. People with this Outer Expression Number tend to overemphasize the seriousness of life. Their capacity for deep contemplation and penetrative analysis, and for the implementation of their high ideals, are fine virtues, but they must be balanced with a little light pleasure to revitalize the mind and body.

Outer Expression 10

Examples of names are Craig, Paul, Shirley, Claude, and Ann—names with consonant number totals of 10, 19, 28, or 37. Outer expression traits indicated by this number are virtually the opposite of those applying to the 9. The inclination to guard against here is that of becoming too flippant and superficial. These people should be more determined to fulfill their role in life, for only by balancing seriousness with lightness will they achieve success.

Outer Expression 11

Examples of names are Allen, Joanne, Kara, and Jonathan—names with consonant number totals of either 11 or 29. The predominant need here is for harmony. This number's special purpose is to instill a desire in these people and others to harmonize surroundings, control emotions, and develop and share a deepened understanding of life.

Outer Expression 22/4

Examples of names are Hamilton and Robert—those few names with a consonant number total of 22 only. This is an exceptionally strong power for organizing, especially in business and commercial ventures. If the person's Ruling Number is a 4, 8, or 22/4, special care must be taken to maintain balance, for the strong leaning here is toward an almost obsessive emphasis on moneymaking. They should endeavor to expand their organizational skills into other ventures by working in such compassionate fields as worthy charities, particularly those benefiting underprivileged children.

Complete Name Numbers

The third aspect of the numerology of names is the key to the name's general strength. This is known as the Complete Name Number. It is related to, but less powerful than, the Ruling Number.

The Complete Name Number is obtained by adding together all the numbers of a name, then totaling them in the same way as was done to obtain the Ruling Number (see Day 9). Remember to use the name you most identify with, whether that is your first name, a nickname, a middle name, or a new name you've chosen to adopt.

Complete Name Numbers range in value from 2 through to 11 and 22/4. The extent of the influence of the Complete Name Number lies in its relationship to the Ruling Number, rather than any specific contribution of its own. A Complete Name Number can either balance or reinforce the power of the Ruling Number. If it is numerically the same as the Ruling Number, it offers the greatest reinforcement. If the Complete Name Number is different from the Ruling Number, but both are on the same Plane (4, 7, and 10 on the Physical Plane; 2, 5, 8, and 11 on the Soul Plane; 3, 6, and 9 on the Mind Plane; and 22/4 both on the Physical and Soul Planes), then balancing reinforcement is given on that Plane.

Finally, if a Complete Name Number is on a different plane from the Ruling Number, a wider range of vibrations is provided for the broadening of the personality.

DAY 21

Compiling Your Name Chart

As we have seen, analyzing the Soul Urge, Outer Expression, and Complete Name Numbers of people's names will provide an understanding of some of the influences that the name provides. Today we are going to learn how to compile a chart of the name, which is similar to that drawn up for the birth date and will unveil further aspects of its contribution to the development of the personality.

The number equivalent of the name's individual letters is placed in its correct space on the chart to show the pattern of the name. To illustrate, we shall use the three sample names of Abraham, Elizabeth, and John, and construct the Name Charts.

```
 1           1       1
 A  B  R  A  H  A  M
    2  9     8     4
```

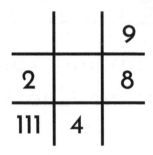

```
 5     9     1     5
 E  L  I  Z  A  B  E  T  H
    3     8     2     2  8
```

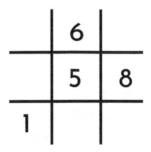

The name pattern is a distinct help in more fully evaluating the personality. When we place the Name Chart beside the Birth Chart, we look for the relationship between them.

Close examination of the juxtaposed Name and Birth Charts shows that there are three possibilities to look for:

• Does the Name Chart offer any strengths that balance weaknesses on the Birth Chart? This is the most desirable function of the Name Chart. If the Name Chart only had one or two numbers on the Soul Plane, this could still provide valuable balance.

• Does the Name Chart intensify any strength already present on the Birth Chart? This creates the most undesirable combination. For instance, if the Name Chart had an abundance of the same numbers as those already appearing on the Birth Chart, there would be too great a concentration of strength. Balance is much more desirable. Remember that the Birth Chart cannot be changed, but the name can.

- Does the name do nothing for the Birth Chart? From time to time this predicament arises. This occurs when a Name Chart cannot offer significant strength to balance weaknesses on the Birth Chart, or when the same weaknesses prevail on both. Often, a slight change in spelling, alteration in length, or interchange of names can provide harmony and balance. Alternatively, a total name change should be considered.

To illustrate with an easy-to-follow example, we shall take one of the names previously used as an illustration, and the birth date of a suitable person—Queen Elizabeth II, born April 21, 1926.

BIRTH CHART

$$2 + 1 + 4 + 1 + 9 + 2 + 6 = 25/7$$

	6	9
22		
11	4	

NAME CHART

5		9		1		5				20/2	
E	L	I	Z	A	B	E	T	H			43/7
	3		8		2		2	8		23/5	

3		9
22	55	88
1		

PYRAMIDS

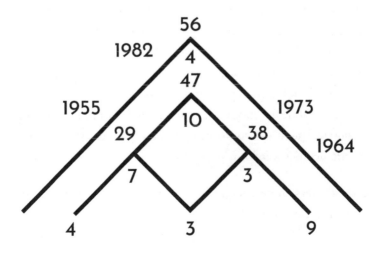

The most noticeable similarity is that her Ruling Number and Complete Name Number are both 7. This strengthens the Ruling Number, indicating the need to undergo many personal sacrifices in early years in order to attain a level of self-control, as well as an ability to impart guidance to others.

The plane of strongest expression here is the Spiritual Plane. It indicates balanced intuition and sensitivity (the two 2's on the Birth Chart). Further spiritual strength comes from the Soul Urge and Outer Expression Numbers of the name (2 and 5 respectively), as they are both spiritual numbers.

The Mind Plane of Queen Elizabeth II's Birth Chart is also strong and well balanced, for though it lacks the 3, it is compensated for by her Day Number 3. Added mental balance is indicated by the top line of her Name Chart.

Her combination of mental and spiritual balance, together with her capacity for self-expression (indicated by the two 1's on her Birth Chart), disclose her natural ease in communicating what and how much she wished to reveal, but her Ruling Number 7 and Complete Name Number 7 indicate that she had much to learn about what should and should not be said in public. She found conforming difficult because she felt that it curtailed her freedom.

Her strongest inherent guidance derived from her intuition. This is reinforced by the two 2's on her Name Chart.

It will be helpful to students of numerology to observe some further points of importance regarding Queen Elizabeth II's personality.

Ruling 7 people are among the most truthful and honest. Queen Elizabeth took her position as "protector of the faith" very seriously, employing uncompromising sincerity to try to live up to the ethics of her church. Hypocrisy was abhorrent to her, so the conflicts within her family must have upset her greatly. Such disharmony was felt very deeply by the Queen due to her strong sense of family responsibility (indicated by the 6 and 9 together without a 3 on her Birth Chart).

So many factors about the Queen's charts and Pyramids indicate that her life was a very serious business. She had little time or patience for flippancy. Her strong Soul Plane and the numbers about the peaks of her Pyramids show that she was a person who would never shirk her responsibilities. In fact, the 9 as the last number on the base of her Pyramids indicates that she had more responsibilities to face in the final stage of her life.

Her intuition (the double 2's) combined with the Ruling Number 7 and Complete Name Number 7 is a reliable indicator of her approach to making decisions. No doubt many of the Queen's advisers complained that she did not consult them as often as she should have. In her mind, she did not need to, and her maturity was so well developed that she could probably have provided more guidance to her advisers than they to her!

The doubling of the 1's and 2's on her Birth Chart indicate how capably Queen Elizabeth II could appreciate other people's viewpoints. She could readily comprehend both sides of a contentious matter—an important attribute when dealing with public figures, especially politicians.

The seriousness of her regal position occupied so much of Queen Elizabeth's thoughts that she needed encouragement to allow some diversion into her life. Prince Philip, with his highly developed sense of humor, was especially helpful in this regard. With his encouragement, the Queen did not take long to discover her "other" self through her Day Number 3. The further influence of her Outer Expression Number 5 reveals that she enjoyed light entertainment and liked to indulge in that enjoyment from time to time.

An analysis of Prince Philip's name and date of birth (June 10, 1921) provides an excellent exercise for the student. From this, it can be seen how much dedicated support he gave to the Queen and how much it assisted her to ease so graciously into her position in public life. It also become clear how well suited the Queen and her husband were. Without his support, her acute sensitivity could have led Queen Elizabeth to become withdrawn.

This is not intended to be an exhaustive analysis, but rather an indication of the interrelationship between the various aspects of numerology. Queen Elizabeth II was chosen as an example because of her worldwide fame and single name. Under normal circumstances, we have at least two names to analyze for a person (the first name and surname). If they are in show business or have taken a pseudonym for professional reasons, we must also analyze those to ascertain the relationships between the various names as well as the birth date characteristics.

From our analysis, it is clear how helpful the name Elizabeth was to the Queen. When we analyze successful people, we find this to be a consistent fact: almost without exception, their name will be in harmony with, and a source of strength to, their natal powers.

Many people overlook the influence exerted by their name on the overall expression of their personality, but names are not given to us by chance or by accident. They attach themselves to us according to our need, though we are rarely aware of this. Parents will choose a name for their child guided by some preference. What created that preference? Nothing occurs by chance—there is always a reason, whether we are aware of it or not. Numerologically, we can reveal that reason and, in so doing, we discover a deeper side to our personality.

Afterword

None of us is born perfect. Hence our purpose here is to evolve toward perfection. And when we become aware of how this can be achieved, we realize that we need to stay here a long time to fulfill such a mission, rather than waste time in successive reacquaintances with our physical bodies and this planet's unique spectrum of vibrations. This is where we definitely have a choice—to grow a little each lifetime or to stay here and get it all done, making the very best of what we have.

Staying on the karmic wheel requires little choice—we just keep doing what we have always done. But to make the momentous decision to stay here until our growth has been completed demands enormous strength of fortitude, temperance, awareness, and courage. It also demands maintaining our body in a state of optimum health so that it can continue to function as the noble messenger for the soul's evolution. All this requires expanding knowledge of our physical, mental, and spiritual selves, an awareness of which numerology can provide a vital key.

As I hope I have shown, numerology is also an intensely practical system designed to provide a unique insight into human personality and its potential, but it is much more than that. It is a valuable means whereby our intuition and other abilities can develop and improve our lives.

Are you ready for the exciting experiences that will now accompany life?

I look forward to sharing the journey with you, but remember as we travel, it is not the way the wind is blowing that determines our progress—over that we have no control; progress is only achieved by the way we set our sails.

About the Author

David A. Phillips (1934–1993) was regarded as one of the world's leading numerologists and was the author of 12 books. His expertise in health and nutrition culminated in his attainment of a doctorate in philosophy from London University in 1971. He travelled regularly to lecture and consult on numerology, incorporating his lifelong study of health and personal growth into his teachings.

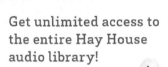